HEROES AND WARRIORS

Chief Joseph

GUARDIAN OF THE NEZ PERCE

JASON HOOK

Plates by RICHARD HOOK

Firebird Books

Acknowledgements

Many thanks to Badger and Dawn Kirby

First published in the UK 1989 by Firebird Books
P.O. Box 327, Poole, Dorset BH15 2RG

Copyright © 1989 Firebird Books Ltd
Text copyright © 1989 Jason Hook

Distributed in the United States by
Sterling Publishing Co, Inc
387 Park Avenue South, New York, NY 10016–8810

Distributed in Australia by
Capricorn Link (Australia) Pty Ltd
P.O. Box 665, Lane Cove, NSW 2066

British Library Cataloguing in Publication Data

Hook, Jason
   Chief Joseph: guardian of the Nez Perce —— (Heroes and warriors)
   1. Pacific Northwest. Nez Perce. Joseph. Nez Perce, Chief
   I. Title II. Series
   979.5'00497

ISBN   1 85314 015 5 (paperback)
ISBN   1 85314 026 0 (cased)

Series editor Stuart Booth
Designed by Kathryn S.A. Booth
Typeset by Inforum Typesetting, Portsmouth
Monochrome origination by Castle Graphics, Frome
Colour separations by Kingfisher Facsimile
Colour printed by Barwell Colour Print (Midsomer Norton)
Printed and bound in Great Britain at The Bath Press

Chief Joseph

GUARDIAN OF THE NEZ PERCE

Studio portrait of Chief Joseph in 1877 when he was 37 years old. He wears blanket coat and leggings, cotton shirt, loop necklaces and moccasins, with his hair in ornamented plaits and the usual swept-up fringe. A fur quiver is visible to Joseph's right, held by a thin strap across his chest.

Route of the Nez Perce on their epic 1,700-mile march from the Wallowa Valley to the Bear Paws, showing the major battles fought during their flight.

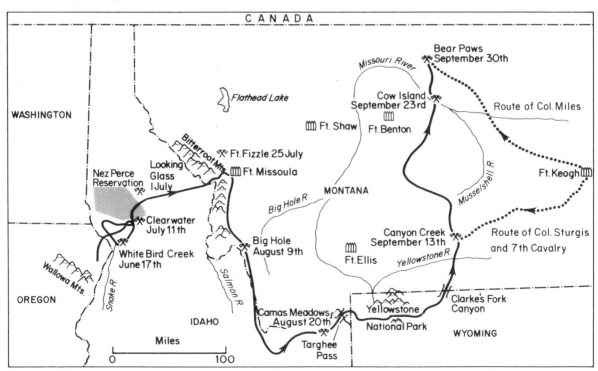

4

The Earth was created by the assistance of the sun, and it should be left as it was. . . .
The country was made without lines of demarcation and it is no man's business to divide
it. . . .

(Chief Joseph)

The whites told only one side. Told it to please themselves. Told much that is not true.
Only his own best deeds, only the worst deeds of the Indians, has the white man told.

(Yellow Knife of the Nez Perce)

Protector of the People

The story of the Nez Perce struggle to defend their ancient homeland is
one of the most outstanding in American history. Proudly, they maintained peace with the white men for seventy years, until finally they
became forced to take up arms, the reluctant tormentors of the US
Army. Yet the spirit, dignity and skill which characterised their struggle
won the Nez Perce many supporters, even among the white communi-
ties.

The Plateau culture region.

Their leader was Chief Joseph, a truly remarkable man. In an era of
violent conflict, his long struggle for peace with the white man remains
one of the most inspiring stories of the time. Thereafter, his leadership of
the Nez Perce, reluctantly into war, was magnificent. Though outnum-
bered the Nez Perce fought valiantly in a gallant but vain attempt to
reach Canada and to find sanctuary. Their journey was a battling retreat,
one of the greatest in all of military history.

The final defeat of the Nez Perce – almost in sight of their goal – and
their surrender, inspired Joseph's greatest adversary to befriend him. In
doing so, General Nelson Miles' own words tell everything about the
nature of Chief Joseph and his brave people:

The boldest and best marksmen of any Indians I have ever encountered. And Chief
Joseph was a man of more sagacity and intelligence than any Indian I have ever met.

Though Joseph spent much of his later life in exile from his beloved
Wallowa Valley, he was never subjugated, possessing a kind dignity that
was as powerful as his leadership when young. The absence of any
atrocities or aggressive acts on the part of Joseph's people sets the Nez
Perce conflict apart from all of the other Indian wars. Its character was
summarised by Joseph's warning to the defenders of Fort Fizzle in Montana:

We are going by you without fighting, if you will let us; but we are going by you
anyhow.

5

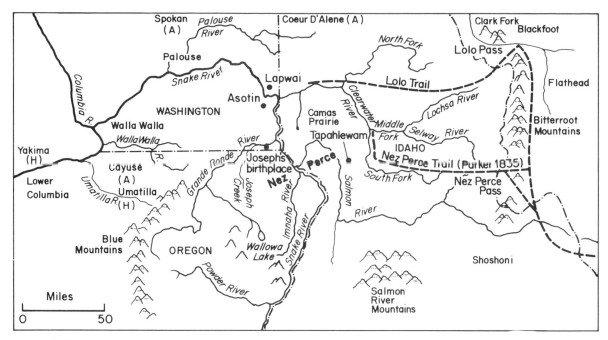

Homeland of the Nez Perce and the neighbouring tribes of the Shahaptian (H) and Salish (A) families that shared their Plateau culture.

The Nez Perce

The Nez Perce, in common with most North American Indian tribes, referred to themselves simply as 'The People' – Nimipu. Their first white visitors, William Clark and Meriwether Lewis, who 'discovered' the tribe in 1805, called them the Chopunnish. This name was probably a corruption of an old Nez Perce word *Tssop-nit-palu*, meaning 'The Walking People'. The explorers also called them 'Pierced Noses', since some of the tribe demonstrated a coastal trait of inserting dentalium through their noses. French trappers adopted this name, translating it to *Nez Percés*, which has been corrupted in English to their modern name of Nez Perces, or simply Nez Perce.

Homelands and Origins

Numbering less than 6000 souls, the Nez Perce roamed a traditional Plateau homeland of some 27,000 square miles, spanning western Idaho, south-eastern Washington, and north-eastern Oregon. A region of lush prairies, sheltered river valleys, towering highlands and precipitous canyons, it spanned the Clearwater Mountains in the north and Salmon River Mountains in the south. The Bitterroots formed their eastern borders, the Blue Mountains and Columbia River their western.

Settlement was concentrated in fishing villages on the tributaries of the Snake, Clearwater and Salmon Rivers. Each village had a headman, but tribal cohesion was apparent only in such co-operative ventures as organising large war, hunting or gathering parties.

6

They were a very bright and energetic body of Indians; indeed the most intelligent that I had ever seen. Exceedingly self-reliant, each man seemed to be able to do his own thinking and to be purely democratic and independent in his ideas and purposes.

(Col. Nelson Miles)

Archaeological remains indicate that the Nez Perce's ancestors occupied caves in the region over 8000 years ago. However, the Nez Perce themselves placed their origins in the blood of a mythical monster slain by the culture hero Coyote. They were the most powerful in the Shahaptian family, which also included the Palouse, Walla Walla, Umatilla, Wanapum, Klickitat, Yakima and Cayuse tribes. Their Plateau culture was shared also by the Salish family of tribes to the north, which included the Salish (Flathead), Spokan, Skitswish (Coeur d'Alênes), Kalispel (Pend D'Oreilles), Okanogan, Sans Poil, Colville, Senijextee (Lake), Ntlakyapamuk, Lilooet, Shuswap, Columbia, Methow and Wenatchee. The Nez Perce feuded with the Spokan and Skitswish, but their most bitter enemies were the Shoshoni, Bannock and Paiute tribes of the Great Basin region to the south.

The People

The Nez Perce were renowned as great travellers, especially following their acquisition of horses in the early eighteenth century. According to legend, their magnificent horse-herds were descended from a white mare and her colt, purchased with dentalium by a peace delegation to

Nez Perce toy cradleboard, front and back, of buckskin-covered board with beadwork decoration and buckskin fringe and carrying strap.

Flathead woman and child, painted by Paul Kane around 1850. The cradleboard is designed to compress the child's skull, creating the flattened head seen on the mother. The Nez Perce borrowed this trait, along with their nose piercing from their original neighbours among the North West Coast tribes.

The distinctively marked Appaloosa ponies – the 'spotted horses' – took their name from the Palouse Indians, but were especially bred by the Nez Perce. They were used in the desperate flight of Joseph and his people.

the Shoshoni. The animals thrived in the rich grasslands, and by 1750 had become central to Nez Perce life. The tribe developed a unique aptitude for horse-breeding, and Meriwether Lewis described them as having a method of gelding 'preferable to that practiced by ourselves'. Through selective breeding, the Nez Perce produced thousands of outstanding horses, including the magnificent Appaloosa ponies – the famous 'spotted horse'.

The mounted Nez Perce developed far greater contact with distant tribes. Westward trips to the Dalles increased in frequency, improving trade with North-west Coast tribes like the Yakima, and introducing to the tribe such coastal traits as nose-piercing and the artificial flattening of babies' heads. More importantly, mounted hunters followed the Lolo and Old Nez Perce trails east over the Bitterroots, and joined bands of Flathead and even Crow in hunting buffalo on the Plains. The Nez Perce hunters carried with them trade goods of dried fish and roots, craftwork of basketry and horn, and shells obtained at the Dalles. They returned laden with buffalo robes and meat, as well as Plains-style costume and artefacts such as magnificent eagle-feather war-bonnets. In this way, the Nez Perce developed a distinctive culture fused from their own traditions and those of the Plains and North-west Coast. This fusion was reflected in their unique ability to communicate in both the sign language of the Plains tribes, and the Chinook trade jargon of the coastal peoples.

New Wars and Weapons

Returning from the buffalo country, Nez Perce warriors boasted of battles with strange peoples: the Blackfoot and Gros Ventre of Canada, the Assiniboin and Crow of the central Plains. Soon the Nez Perce were participating in Plains-style warfare, raiding for horses, and for scalps when their own herds were stolen. Scouts led war-parties over great distances to the camps of their enemies. Before entering battle, the warriors stripped to breech-cloth and moccasins, some donning war-bonnets, then prepared their medicine bundles and applied sacred body paint to invoke the *Wyakin* medicine powers that gave them supernatural protection. Before they acquired firearms in the first years of the

Nez Perce war-bonnet of 1860–90. It is constructed from eagle feathers, horse-hair, red cloth, ermine pendants, buffalo-horn strips, beadwork and brass bells. Such headdresses denoted accomplished warriors and were adopted from the Plains tribes.

nineteenth century, the Nez Perce fought with clubs, lances and their most famous weapon, a bow of mountain sheep horn. The curled horn was boiled until pliable, stretched and straightened, then backed with deer sinew attached with a glue of salmon skin or sturgeon blood. The horn bow's power and beauty was worth the trade of a good horse on the Plains.

About 1755, the Blackfoot obtained firearms from the Hudson's Bay Company, and drove back the Shoshoni and Flathead, so exposing the Bitterroot valley. Allying themselves with neighbouring tribes, the Nez Perce thwarted Blackfoot aggression in a period of desperate warfare. By 1800, Nez Perce buffalo-hunting expeditions to the Yellowstone had become too dangerous, and five years later a council in the Kamiah valley resolved to obtain firearms for the tribe. Three warriors from the band of Chief Broken Arm (Tunnachemootoolt) made a perilous journey of some 1000 miles, beyond the lands of the Teton Sioux, to trade with the Hidatsa Indians. Incredibly, they returned safely, bearing the first six firearms among the Nez Perce. The Lewis and Clark expedition was able to provide powder and lead for the Nez Perce, a persuasive enough argument for their friendly relations with the white man.

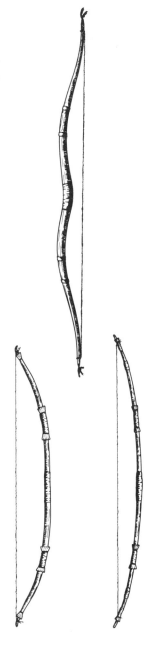

Among the Nez Perce and Crow people, pieces of horn were glued together and bound with sinew to create a bow 'stronger, tougher, more elastic, and more durable than a bow of any other materials'. The horn bow was a popular weapon among the Nez Perce both for its power and beauty.

Corps of Discovery

According to tribal legend, the first Nez Perce to encounter a white man was a woman called Watkuweis, meaning 'Returned from a Faraway Country'. Captured by Blackfoot or Atsina Indians when accompanying buffalo-hunters to Montana in the late eighteenth century, she was sold to eastern Indians and then on to a French-Canadian at Red River. After giving birth to a child, Watkuweis ran away and journeyed back to her own people. She spoke kindly of the white men, whom she called Soyappo ('Long Knives') and when William Clark first entered the Nez Perce lands, Watkuweis, now aged and dying, apparently told her tribe: 'These are the people who helped me. Do them no hurt'.

The Lewis and Clark expedition, the Corps of Discovery, first entered the Bitterroot Mountains on 11th September 1805, seeking the Columbia River. A week later, they recorded reaching the 'Kooskooske' River, from the Nez Perce *Koos keich keich*, meaning Clearwater. Here Clark led six men ahead to secure much needed supplies. At the Nez Perce camp on Weippe prairie, and later in the Clearwater valley, the expedition met only kindness and help from the Nez Perce. Thus, Lewis and Clark left the area with a strong regard for the Nez Perce:

Among the most amiable men we have seen. Their character is placid and gentle, rarely moved into passion.

(Meriwether Lewis)

9

Bow-case and quiver, probably Nez Perce, of otterskin decorated with beadwork and pendants of ermine. Like many other aspects of Nez Perce design, it demonstrates a strong Crow influence.

Long Knives and Black Robes

In May 1806, Lewis and Clark re-entered the Nez Perce homeland, on their journey back from the Pacific. The previous summer they had left an American flag for Broken Arm, who had been absent leading a triumphant attack on the Shoshoni. Now, they presented all the Nez Perce headmen with medals. Then, through a series of interpreters, they called for the Nez Perce to cease making war upon other tribes, so that a trading post could be established. After witnessing a demonstration of 'magnetism, the spye glass, compass, watch, airgun and sundry other items', Broken Arm consented to this request. The other headmen indicated their agreement by attending a feast given by the chief, though the women of the village 'cried, wrung their hands, tore their hair, and appeared to be in the utmost distress', at the notion of this fundamental change to tribal life.

However, an elderly man assured the expedition of the tribe's 'warmest attachment and that they would always give them every assistance in their power; that they were poor but their hearts were good'. This tribal promise was the cornerstone of the Nez Perce's determined and continued friendship with the white man.

In July, the Nez Perce guided Lewis and Clark along the Lolo Trail and out of their lands, after receiving assurances that American traders would be sent to their country. Travelling east, Lewis encountered two men, Joseph Dixon and Forrest Hancock, trapping the Missouri west from Illinois. They were the vanguard of a legion of trappers, traders and mountain men who would pioneer American settlement of the far West. In December that year, Nez Perce traded at Kootenae House for the first time, and by 1810 they had obtained sufficient firearms to join the Flathead in a party of 150 that drove back the Blackfoot, whose hostility had plagued initial efforts of traders to penetrate westward.

In 1811, the ragged remnants of an expedition from John Jacob Astor's Pacific Fur Company sought refuge among the Nez Perce, and were guided safely to Fort Astoria on the lower Columbia. Among them was Donald Mackenzie, a 312-pound colossus, who returned the following year to build Fort Nez Perce on the confluence of the Snake and Clearwater Rivers. Mackenzie expected to exchange trade goods for beaver skins, but the Nez Perce refused to trap beaver, since it was not consistent with their seasonal existence. Mackenzie's men had to set the traps themselves. Then, when their supplies ran short, they had to exchange trade goods with the Nez Perce for horse-meat.

On 16th October 1813, the Pacific Fur Company sold out to the North West traders, having pushed relations with the Indians to their limit.

Mackenzie returned to Astoria, now Fort George, in 1816 and secured employment with the North West Company. Having councilled with the Nez Perce for two years, in July 1818, he re-established a fort in their name in the region of the Cayuse and Walla Walla Indians. For four years

he led beaver-trapping expeditions along the Snake with increasing success, while the Nez Perce warriors confined themselves to fleecing the less provident of Mackenzie's Iroquois henchmen. Mackenzie made futile attempts to negotiate a peace between the Nez Perce and the Shoshoni before his departure in 1821, when the North West and Hudson's Bay Companies were merged. Two years later, the traders' annihilation of a Piegan Blackfoot war-party cemented relations with the Nez Perce.

Between 1824 and 1830, the Nez Perce switched their allegiance from the British to the growing bands of free-spirited American mountain men, who traded generously and treated the Indians as equals. In 1832 at the Pierre's Hole rendezvous, the Nez Perce fought a long and decisive battle alongside the Americans against some transient Blackfoot. Twenty-five Blackfoot warriors were killed, while two Nez Perce chiefs were injured. They were Rotten Belly (Tackensautis) and Hallalhotsoot, called Lawyer by the Americans because of his shrewd diplomacy.

In February 1834, an American called Benjamin Bonneville penetrated

Headman Bull's Head with wife and dog travois. The Nez Perce absorbed much of the culture of the Plains, where the travois was used before the introduction of the horse.

the lower Nez Perce heartland west of the Snake in the continuing battle to win over trade from the British. Bonneville, called the 'Bald Headed Chief' by the Indians, visited the Asotin band of Nez Perce, where he administered medicine to the daughter of Flint Necklace, or Old Looking Glass, father of Chief Joseph's greatest ally. He also visited a settlement on Joseph Creek, on the Grande Ronde, whose headman was Chief Joseph's father, Tuekakas.

The 1834 Green River rendezvous was attended both by Nez Perce headmen and the burly, broad-jawed Methodist minister Jason Lee. His presence was transient, but other 'Black Robes' were shortly to follow in his footsteps. An interest in Christianity had first arisen among the Nez Perce when a Spokan and a Kutenai boy returned after four years at the Red River Church of England Mission School. Dressed as white men, speaking English and clutching bible and prayer-book in their hands, Spokan Garry and Kutenai Pelly caused a sensation. After meeting them, Nez Perce headmen including Lawyer and Timothy dispatched a delegation to St Louis in late summer 1831 to answer claims that 'the white man's religion was better than theirs, and that they would all be lost if they did not embrace it' (Catlin).

In May 1835, the pompous, purse-lipped Presbyterian minister Samuel Parker and his zealous assistant Dr Marcus Whitman left Liberty for Oregon, predicting that the 'Church-going bell will sound far and wide'.

Dispatching Whitman back east for reinforcements, Parker travelled extensively beyond the Salmon River Mountains, before reaching Fort Vancouver. He conducted sermons, and met many Nez Perce headmen, including Tuekakas, of whom he wrote: 'If there is one among this multitude who it may be hoped has been everlastingly benefitted by the gospel, I should believe it is this man'. Of the Nez Perce, Parker observed: 'I have nowhere witnessed so much subordination, peace and friendship as among the Indians in the Oregon Territory. The day may be rued when their order and harmony shall be interrupted by any instrumentality whatever.'

In July 1836, Whitman and his new wife Narcissa, accompanied by the stern, short-tempered Reverend Henry Spalding and his ailing spouse Eliza, hauled a wagon over what would become the Oregon Trail, to Fort Vancouver. While Whitman established his mission among the Cayuse, the Spaldings ventured 120 miles east to Lapwai, 'Place of Butterflies', on the Clearwater, where their mission grew slowly.

In July 1839, Spalding travelled to the village of Tuekakas – who became known as Old Joseph – in the beautiful Wallowa valley. Here he baptised and conducted Christian marriages for Old Joseph and his wife Khapkhaponimi (Asenoth), and for Tamootsin (Timothy) and his wife Tamar. Then on 12th April 1840, he baptised Old Joseph's newborn baby 'Ephraim', who as an adult would inherit his father's name, Joseph.

Thunder Travelling to Distant Mountains

Joseph was born in the spring of 1840 in a cave near where Joseph Creek forks from the Grande Ronde River. Here, the Wellamotkin band of Nez Perce sheltered from winter snows in a village of tipis and circular pit-houses, centred on a large, rectangular council lodge, its floor dug below ground, its roof an A-shaped frame covered with tule mats. After the wildflowers blossomed in March, they journeyed south along the lush Wallowa valley to gather wild roots like kouse and camas.

Christian Childhood

After being baptised in the hands of Henry Spalding, Joseph spent much of his first seven years at the Lapwai Mission, where Eliza Spalding's growing band of helpers gave academic and religious instruction. During this time, Henry Spalding drove a wedge into the Nez Perce tribe, dividing them into Christians, who followed his preaching, and the 'heathen' faction, who maintained their traditional beliefs. This rent in the tribal fabric was torn wider by Dr Elijah White, Superintendent of Indian Affairs, who presented the Nez Perce with a set of rules to govern them, and demanded that they appoint a head chief. He selected Ellis, grandson of Red Grizzly Bear, a choice which angered Lawyer and Joseph and created more problems than it solved.

The increase in white settlement on the Columbia, which saw 3000 newcomers in 1845, led to growing fears among both Christian and 'heathen factions' of the Nez Perce. These matured in 1847, when wagons carried 4000 people along the Oregon Trail, along with an epidemic of measles. Over half the Cayuse tribe died, and while Whitman treated those he could, the rumour spread that the missionary was, in fact, poisoning the Indians. On the afternoon of 29th November 1847,

Nez Perce shield and cover of 1870. Made from buffalo hide and deerskin, it is decorated with eagle feathers. The original red, yellow and blue paint designs reflected the owner's medicine and his vision-spirit, the deer.

Cayuse chief Tilokaikt appeared at Whitman's home. He asked the doctor for some medicine, then as Whitman turned to fetch it, felled him with a tomahawk. In the ensuing massacre, eleven men, Narcissa Whitman and two children were savagely killed and forty-seven people captured, later to be ransomed.

Spalding, after being warned of his peril by Catholic priest Father Brouillet, fled from the massacre to Lapwai. On New Year's Day of 1848, friendly Nez Perce escorted him out of their lands to Fort Walla Walla. The Cayuse War raged from 1847 to 1850, in which year the Whitman Massacre ringleaders were hung, and the Indians' lands opened to homesteading by the Oregon Donation Land Law. Although Protestant missionaries were banned from the region, converts such as Lawyer and Timothy maintained the faith; by 1860 the Christian faction comprised two-thirds of the tribe.

Learning the Old Ways

Old Joseph retired to the seclusion of the Wallowa valley to escape the soldiers that marched through his country, but with whom he had no direct quarrel. Here, his son Joseph learnt the traditions and religion of his own people. The Nez Perce believed in an infinite number of spirits, all of them a part of one omnipotent deity and embodying a sacred Wyakin power, which was present in the land, elements and animals of their country. At the age of nine, Joseph was instructed by a holy man on how to attain his own guardian spirit or *Wyakin*. In the following years, he would have undertaken a vision quest similar to that described by the Nez Perce warrior Yellow Wolf:

I was a boy of about thirteen snows when my parents sent me away into the hills . . . to find my Wyakin. After going so many suns without food, I was sleeping. It was just like dreaming what I saw. A form stood in the air fronting me . . . . It was a Spirit of a wolf that appeared to me. Yellow-like in colour it sort of floated in the air. Like a human-being it talked to me – and gave me its power . . . . That was how I got named Yellow Wolf.

The recipient of a *Wyakin* participated in the winter ceremonial Guardian Spirit Dance, where he sang the medicine song taught by his *Wyakin*.

From his uncle, Joseph received the name Hin-mah-too-yah-lat-kekht, 'Thunder Travelling to Distant Mountains'. His younger brother, born two years after him, was named Ollokot – Frog – after a half-brother of Old Joseph. While Ollokot was boisterous and full of daring, the young Joseph demonstrated the gentle, dignified nature that would distinguish his later life.

Council at Walla Walla

When he was fifteen, Joseph travelled with his father to the Walla Walla valley, where Isaac I. Stevens, governor of newly formed Washington Territory and Superintendent of Indian Affairs, had called one of a series of treaty councils removing Indian land rights. On 24th May 1855, Lawyer, Old Joseph, The Wolf (Utsinmalikin), Three Feathers (Metat Waptass) and Red Wolf (Hemene Ilppilp) led 2500 Nez Perce to the council grounds, where Stevens' 100-strong entourage was camped with other tribes of the Columbia basin. The warriors approached:

Mounted on fine horses and riding at a gallop, two abreast, naked to the breech-clout, their faces covered with white, red and yellow paint in fanciful designs, and decked with plumes and feathers and trinkets fluttering in the sunshine.

They encircled the commissioners, singing and beating shields and drums, before dismounting and conducting a dance.

Prior to the council, Lawyer was given a paper proclaiming him head chief of the Nez Perce. Joseph himself recollected how, on 29th May, Stevens 'made known his heart':

He said that there were a great many white people in the country and many more would come; that he wanted the land marked out so that the Indians and white men could be separated. If they were to live in peace it was necessary, he said, that the Indians should have a country set apart for them and in that country they must stay.

For two weeks, Stevens cajoled the Nez Perce headmen, including Old Joseph, who had clear words for the commissioners:

These are my children. I see them all sitting here. Talking slowly is good. It is good for old men to talk straight; talk straight on both sides and take care of one another. It is not us we talk for, it is for our children who come after us.

Lawyer moved his lodge into the centre of the commissioners' camp and, under his influence, the chiefs seemed ready to sign. Their decision was delayed by the arrival of the formidable war chief of the Asotin band, Old Looking Glass, seventy winters old, at the head of a line of warriors. Brandishing a scalp freshly taken in Blackfoot country, he admonished the Nez Perce headmen:

My people, what have you done? While I was gone, you have sold my country. I have come home and there is not left me a place on which to pitch my lodge. Go home to your lodges. I will talk to you.

However, after a heated discussion, Lawyer's will prevailed; and on 11th June Stevens, calling for no speeches, conducted the treaty signing. Lawyer took up the pen first, followed by Old Looking Glass, Old Joseph, Old James and Timothy, until fifty-eight Nez Perce chiefs were recorded. They accepted $200,000 and a reservation embracing much of their traditional homeland, while retaining the rights to their traditional hunting and fishing grounds. While Joseph returned with his father to the Wallowa, now officially Nez Perce land, a delegation under Old Looking Glass accompanied Stevens to Blackfoot lands. There, in October, they negotiated a remarkable treaty, ending the ancient hostilities between the Blackfoot and the Nez Perce.

Prompted by Stevens' treaty at Walla Walla, there was an immediate

Ceremonial Nez Perce drum which is attributed to Joseph.

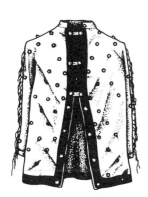

An unusual coat with studded decoration and ermine fringes, accredited to Chief Joseph.

rush east of the Cascades for land and for gold. The Indians were angered by this invasion, and on 29th October Stevens received news that the Yakima, Cayuse, Walla Walla, Umatilla and Palouse Indians had risen against the settlers. The Nez Perce were restrained from joining the conflict by Lawyer and Old Joseph, though frequent outrages perpetrated by troops made up of Oregon volunteers increased support for the war faction under Old Looking Glass. At a second Walla Walla council in September 1856, Stevens found that although the Nez Perce were unwilling to fight, they were clearly divided, largely as a legacy of Spalding's days amongst them. Lawyer's Christian faction upheld the treaty, while Old Joseph denied that he had understood its tenets, and Old Looking Glass failed even to attend. In August 1858, Nez Perce scouts accompanied the punitive expedition of General George Wright, who ruthlessly subdued the tribes of the upper Columbia, hanging prisoners on the spot. As the influx of settlers continued, the Nez Perce now stood alone.

The 1855 treaty was finally ratified in 1859, with Old Joseph commenting: 'The line was made as I wanted it, not for me but my children that will follow me. There is where I live and there is where I want to leave my body'. Such aspirations were threatened in February the following year when one Elias Davidson Pierce discovered gold in the Clearwater. Within a year, 10,000 miners had flocked from the Walla Walla settlement on to the reservation, and Lawyer's followers readily signed an agreement exchanging mining rights north of the Clearwater for $50,000. A military post, Fort Lapwai, was established in 1862, when the Surveyors General Office reported 18,690 whites illegally encamped on the Nez Perce reservation.

In January 1863, Old Looking Glass died and was succeeded by a son of the same name, hanging his father's trade mirror, and his burdens, about his own neck. Old Joseph kept his people away from the miners, and mocked Lawyer as the annuities promised in 1855 failed to arrive. He warned: 'After a while they will claim that you accepted pay for your country'. On 28th April 1862, the *Oregon Statesman* reported:

If open hostilities have not commenced with the Nez Perce it is not because they have not been outraged to that degree when 'forbearance ceases to be a virtue.' In return for the continued friendship in times of want, and generous acts of hospitality always so readily extended towards the whites by these Indians, they now reap an abundant harvest of every species of villainy and insult.

The Thief Treaty

In response to growing friction between the Nez Perce and the miners, Superintendent of Indian Affairs Calvin Hale, escorted by six companies of troops, met with Lawyer's people at Lapwai. Opening the council on 25th May 1863, Hale made the incredible proposal that the Nez Perce sell 90% of their 10,000 square mile reservation, and retire to a 600 square

Joseph leads the Nez Perce warriors in hauling the women and children, clinging together, across the flooded Snake River, May 1877.

mile area on the south fork of the Clearwater. The following day, the wily Lawyer gave his reply, expressing his people's wish:

To adhere to the (1855) treaty that has been made, and which we on our side have kept . . . you have broken the treaty not we . . . That engagement was made with us for 20 years . . . Here we are listening to what you say again, before the 20 years are ended. Perhaps by contemplating you will find something that is wrong in your proposition . . . Dig the gold and look at the country, but we cannot give you the country you ask for.

When the council re-convened on 3rd June, the arrival of the anti-treaty Nez Perce – led by Old Joseph and his son, Big Thunder, Eagle from the Light, Three Feathers, Red Owl and White Bird – had swelled the Indian ranks to 3000. Ignoring the newcomers, Hale coaxed Lawyer and his headmen over to his side by offering them personal guarantees and doubling the size of the proposed reservation. To protect the Lawyer faction, and his own interests, Hale then called up twenty cavalrymen under Captain George Currey. Arriving at 1 a.m., Currey found 53 Nez Perce chiefs gathered in one lodge. He witnessed a remarkable council and duly reported:

Nez Perce gauntlets of around 1890. The unusual altar design probably reflects the Christian church's powerful influence over the tribe.

Chiefs were debating the terms of the proposed treaty in an effort to reach some compromise, but neither group would yield. Finally convinced that there was no hope of agreement, they decided that the proper action was to disband the tribe, each chief becoming an independent leader of his own village . . . (and) declared the Nez Perce nation dissolved. . . . I withdrew my detachment having accomplished nothing but that of witnessing the extinguishment of the last council fires of the most powerful Indian nation on the sunset side of the Rocky Mountains.

Joseph and the other anti-treaty chiefs now struck their lodges and left the council grounds, believing that they had refuted Lawyer's right to speak for them. However, Hale proceeded regardless, and on 9th June 1863, he obtained fifty-two signatures for his treaty. All the signatories were Christians, many were minor headmen and all already lived within the new reservation – except Jason and Timothy, who received provision to live among the whites. Hale accumulated enough names to suggest tribal acceptance despite the absence of every anti-treaty chief. Even old Henry Spalding, who had returned to Lapwai in the spring, added his signature for good measure. Currey noted: 'Although the treaty goes out to the World as the concurrent agreement of the tribe, it is in reality nothing more than the agreement of Lawyer and his band, numbering in the aggregate not a third part of the Nez Perce tribe.'

In the Wallowa valley, Old Joseph tore in two the piece of paper he called the Thief Treaty. He cast aside his 'Book of Heaven', the Bible, and with it any pretence of Christianity. Drawing a map of his people's lands, he then hammered stakes around the Wallowa – creating a boundary that settlers called Old Joseph's Deadline – and made his declaration to his people, but also to his son:

Inside is the home of my people – the white man may take the land outside. Inside the

'We are going by you without fighting if you will let us, but we are going by you anyhow.' Joseph and Looking Glass guide their cavalcade high over Fort Fizzle into Montana, 28th July 1877.

boundary all our people were born. It circles around the graves of our fathers, and we will never give up these graves to any man. When you go into council with the white man, always remember your country. Do not give it away. The white man will cheat you out of your home. I have taken no pay from the United States. I have never sold our land.

Young Joseph, soon to assume the burden of his father's chieftainship, also inherited his father's dignity and wisdom. He summarised the 1863 treaty eloquently:

If we ever owned the land, we own it still, for we never sold it. In the treaty councils the commissioners have claimed that our country has been sold to the government. Suppose a white man should come to me and say 'Joseph, I like your horses, and I want to buy them.' I say to him, 'No, my horses suit me. I will not sell them.' Then he goes to my neighbour and says to him: 'Joseph has some good horses. I want to buy them but he refuses to sell.' My neighbour answers, 'Pay me the money, and I will sell you Joseph's horses.' The white man returns to me and says, 'Joseph, I have bought your horses, and you must let me have them.' If we sold our lands to the Government, this is the way they were bought.

The treaty demanded that, within a year of its being ratified, the Nez Perce should abandon the Wallowa, Grande Ronde, Imnaha, Snake and Salmon valleys, and report on the Lapwai reservation. For this they would receive $315,000. They must have recalled the prophetic remarks in 1829 of the Nez Perce elder Speckled Snake: 'I have listened to many talks from the great father. But they always began and ended in this – Get a little further, you are too near me'.

Nez Perce warrior's sacred wing-bone whistle adorned with buckskin carrying-thong and eagle fluffies. Such whistles were blown only during war to offer the warrior supernatural protection.

Chief Joseph

Before his death at Lapwai in the summer of 1874, Henry Spalding led a Christian revival among the Nez Perce. He recorded over 200 baptisms, including those of Lawyer and Rotten Belly, though some whispered that due to his failing eyesight he baptised certain individuals more than once. The gaping division between the settled, Christian, treaty Nez Perce, and the 'heathen', non-treaty faction was further widened at this time by the appearance of the Dreamer religion, introduced by a hunch-backed Wanapum holy man named Smohalla. After a mysterious five-year absence from his tribe in the 1850s, Smohalla had returned preaching the Dreamer doctrine:

My young men shall never work. Men who work cannot dream; and wisdom comes to us in dreams.

You ask me to plough the ground. Shall I take a knife and tear my mother's breast? Then when I die she will not take me to her bosom to rest.

You ask me to dig for stone. Shall I dig under her skin for bones? Then when I die, I cannot enter her body to be born again.

You ask me to cut grass and make hay and sell it and be rich like white men. But how dare I cut off my mother's hair?

Like the Shawnee prophet Tenskwatawa in 1805, and the Paiute Ghost Dance shaman Wovoka in 1890, Smohalla predicted that a return to traditional life among the Indians would lead to the demise of the white men. This doctrine reflected the beliefs of Young Joseph, whose first wife gave birth to a daughter in 1865. Now twenty-five winters old, Joseph was a powerfully built, strikingly handsome man. Like all the Wallowa Nez Perce, he wore his hair long with a distinctive swept up fringe. This style was characteristic of the Dreamers, and Smohalla's doctrine became increasingly identified with the non-treaty bands.

While white society engulfed the Christian Nez Perce, the 200 or so people of Joseph's Wellamotkin band remained aloof in the Wallowa valley. They wintered in the lush lowlands of canyons on the Grande Ronde and Imnaha valleys, wandering up Joseph Creek in the spring to harvest kouse on the higher meadows. After gathering camas in July, they travelled to the shores of the crystal blue Wallowa Lake, where surrounding streams yielded fat salmon. Here in the Valley of Winding Waters, Joseph was at home. Meanwhile his brother Ollokot, of even larger build and with an unquenchable thirst for life, led buffalo-hunting expeditions to the far off Blackfoot lands. His stature as a war-chief grew in proportion to Joseph's stature as a civil leader. The Wellamotkin also journeyed to the reservation to sell cattle to the Christian Nez Perce. In autumn they hunted deer on Joseph Creek on their return.

Many Nez Perce warriors carried a sacred war-club like this, with a stone head encased in elk rawhide. The handle was wrapped with otter-skin and daubed with paint designs in order to offer the warrior the protection of his vision-spirits.

The Promise

Although over 500 settlers occupied the Grande Ronde valley, the Wallowa remained free from invasion until surveyors, those harbingers of doom among the Indians, arrived in 1866. Joseph's people pulled up the stakes that the surveyors planted, but after the ratification of the Thief Treaty the next year, they continued to arrive.

The first Wallowa settler, A.C. Smith, met the Nez Perce on friendly terms in 1868, returning permanently with cattle and comrades three years later. Old Joseph had by now grown so blind that he rode with a child in his lap to guide him, and so was spared the sight of this first intrusion. In October 1871, the proud old man called his son to his side:

I saw he was dying. I took his hand in mine. He said, 'My son, my body is returning to my mother earth, and my spirit is going very soon to see the Great Spirit. . . . When I am gone, think of your country. You are the chief of these people. They look to you to guide them. Always remember that your father never sold his country. You must stop your ears whenever you are asked to sign a treaty selling your home. A few years more and white men will be all around you. They have their eyes on this land. My son, never forget my dying words. This country holds your father's body. Never sell the bones of your father and your mother.' I pressed my father's hand and told him that I would protect his grave with my life.

(Joseph)

Having guaranteed his homeland's future, Old Joseph, Tuekakas, was buried in the Wallowa. His favourite horse was shot and draped over the grave and a dreamer bell was suspended over the chief's body, to ring in the wind until a white man stole it in 1874. Joseph rode away at the head of his people, seeking shelter from the winter snows, recalling of his father:

I buried him in that beautiful valley of winding waters. I love that land more than all the rest of the world. A man who would not love his father's grave is worse than a wild animal.

Valley of Winding Waters

Returning to the Wallowa in late spring 1872, Joseph found some sixty settlers living in cabins. He immediately made a formal protest and Agent Monteith was summoned to mediate. On 23rd August, at a council of thirty settlers and eighty Nez Perce, many with their faces painted, Joseph made the situation clear to Monteith:

I did not want to come to this council, but I came hoping that we could save blood. The white man has no right to come here and take our country. We have never accepted presents from the government. Neither Lawyer nor any other chief had authority to sell this land. It has always belonged to my people. It came unclouded to them from our fathers, and we will defend this land, as long as a drop of Indian blood warms the hearts of our men.

Monteith received Joseph's guarantee that the settlers would not be molested, but noted in his report:

It is a great pity that the valley was ever opened for settlement. It is so high and cold that they can raise nothing but the hardiest kind of vegetables . . . it is the only fishery the Nez Perces have and they go there from all directions. . . . If there is any way by which the Wallowa Valley could be kept for the Indians I would recommend that it be done.

In response to Monteith's report, the Secretary of the Interior dispatched T.B. Odeneal, Superintendent of Indian Affairs for Oregon, to meet Joseph on 27th March 1873. Odeneal was swayed by the eloquence and truth of Joseph's argument, and submitted a practical solution. He recommended that the 'upper' country, meaning the highlands east of and including Wallowa Lake, be granted to the Nez Perce; and the 'lower' country, meaning the westerly Grande Ronde valley where white settlers were concentrated, remain open to settlement.

In June, President Grant issued an executive order establishing a Wallowa Reservation 'for the roaming Nez Perce Indians', which bore no relation to Odeneal's recommendations. The Bureau of Indian Affairs, making no reference to the actual territory, had translated Odeneal's 'upper' as north, and 'lower' as south, and divided the land laterally instead of vertically. The Nez Perce received the settled lands to the north, while the settlers received the Wallowa Lake region so treasured and traversed by the Indians. The alarmed settlers immediately formed themselves into a blustering militia, and Lafayette F. Grover,

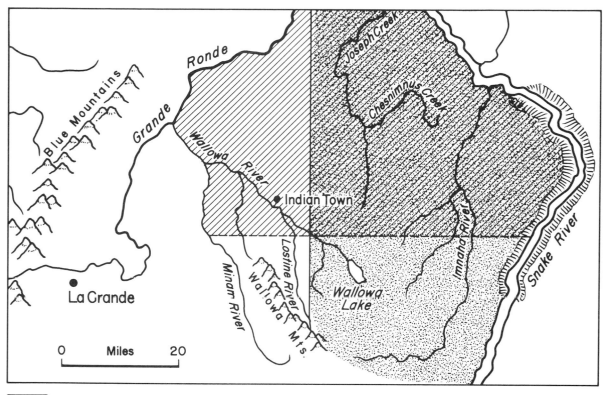

Wanted by the Wallowa Nez Perce

Wallowa Reservation as set up by the Commissioners in 1873

The part of the Wallowa Valley desired by the Nez Perce in 1873, and the completely contradictory area allocated them by the Indian Bureau. In fact, the Bureau translated 'upper' and 'lower' to mean north and south, and thus divided the land in ignorance of its true topography and contours.

Joseph's ceremonial robe and Winchester rifle, which are now in the Fort Benton Museum.

Governor of Oregon, successfully petitioned the Secretary of the Interior to re-examine the situation, declaring: 'Joseph's band do not desire Wallowa Valley for a reservation and for a home. This small band wish the possession of this large section of Oregon simply for room to gratify a wild, roaming disposition, and not for a home.'

At the beginning of August, Joseph was summoned to Lapwai by yet another commission desiring his settlement at an agency. He was asked if his people wanted schools: 'No, we do not want schools . . . they will teach us to have churches. : They [churches] will teach us to quarrel about God. We do not want to learn that. We may quarrel with men sometimes about things on this earth, but we never quarrel about God. We do not want to learn that'.

In September, Joseph requested permission to travel to Washington to correct the mistakes made in the recent settlement. Agent Monteith refused it, pressured by the settlers' supporters and frustrated by the Wallowa band's reluctance to farm. 'Nearly every year,' Joseph recalled, 'the agent came over from Lapwai and ordered us on to the reservation. We always replied that we were satisfied to live in Wallowa. We were careful to refuse the presents or annuities which he offered.'

On 18th May 1874, Commissioner of Indian Affairs E.P. Smith informed Oregon Senator James Kelly that 'the whole (Wallowa) valley is now open for settlement'. Two months later, there was an inconclusive exchange of shots between a Nez Perce and one of the settlers. Encouraged by Lawyer, Monteith responded by stationing troops on Weippe Prairie and on the Wallowa, where the Nez Perce and Umatilla fished for salmon. When the troops withdrew in October, the anti-treaty Nez Perce met in council at Tepahlewam (Split Rocks), an age-old meeting place on Camas Prairie. Representing their bands were Joseph and Ollokot from the Wallowa; Red Owl (Koolkool Snehee) and Looking Glass from the Middle Fork of the Clearwater; White Bird from the Salmon River; and a powerful warrior, holy man and orator named Toohoolhoolzote from the Snake River region. After addresses by Looking Glass, Red Owl and the renowned warriors Rainbow (Wahchumyus), Five Wounds (Pahkatos Owyeen) and Grizzly Bear Ferocious, the Nez Perce voted against war. The decision pleased Joseph, who later lamented:

Our young men were quick-tempered, and I have had great trouble in keeping them from doing rash things. I have carried a heavy load on my back ever since I was a boy. I learned then that we were but few, while the white men were many, and that we could not hold our own with them. We were like deer. They were like grizzly bears. We had a small country. Their country was large. We were contented to let things remain as the Great Spirit . . . made them. They were not, and would change the rivers and mountains if they did not suit them.

On 10th June 1875, President Grant rescinded his 1873 executive order, officially re-opening the entire Wallowa valley for settlement.

The Death of Wilhautyah

Leading a band of forty-five lodges up the Valley of Winding Waters in the summer of 1875, Joseph found two companies of cavalry under Captain Whipple stationed there as a peace-keeping force. The troops returned to Fort Walla Walla in September, but were recalled to the valley on New Year's Day by reports that Joseph's Nez Perce were murdering the settlers. After battling through four-feet snow drifts, the soldiers discovered that Joseph was, in fact, peacefully visiting the Lapwai agency, some 100 miles from the imagined outrages.

In January 1876, the one-armed General Oliver Otis Howard, Commander of the Department of the Columbia, received a commissioned report from Major H.C. Wood which concluded: 'The non-treaty Nez Perces cannot in law be regarded as bound by the treaty of 1863; and in so far as it attempts to deprive them of a right to occupancy on any land its provisions are null and void.'

The one-armed, 'Praying General' Oliver Otis Howard predicted of his campaign against the Nez Perce: 'Think we will make short work of it'. However, Howard's quarry, Chief Joseph, after frequently and comprehensively out-manoeuvring him, soon re-named him 'General Day After Tomorrow'.

However, such considerations were overshadowed by an incident five months later. A settler called A.B. Findley tracked five missing horses to the Chesnimnus region, where Wallowa Indians were gathering roots. He returned the following day, the 23rd June, with 21-year-old Wells McNall, a renowned Indian-hater, and confronted three Nez Perce. In the ensuing argument, McNall began to wrestle with a young Nez Perce named Wilhautyah (Wind Blowing) for possession of the Indian's gun. Weakening, McNall bellowed at Findley to open fire. Eventually he did, shooting Wilhautyah dead. The two white men fled back to the settlements.

When Wilhautyah's body was carried into his camp, Joseph urged restraint from his angry warriors. Hurrying to Lapwai, he received Monteith's assurance that the white men would be brought to justice before returning to his people. On 22nd July, Major Wood came to the Wallowa to investigate the killing, and reported Joseph as saying that 'the valley was more sacred to him than ever before, and he would and did claim it now as recompense for the life taken.' Despite Wood's assurances that Findley and McNall would be tried, they remained at large in the valley. Joseph complained: 'We had no friend who would plead our cause before the law councils'. The Nez Perces' patience wore thin.

On 1st September, Nez Perce warriors in ugly mood summoned the Wallowa settlers to a council the following day. When it convened, Joseph instructed the white men to leave the valley, and turn over Findley and McNall to the Nez Perce for trial. Leading sixty warriors stripped for battle to McNall's cabin, where several families had fortified themselves, Joseph repeated his warning.

The settlers dispatched messengers to warn their comrades and seek help. One of them, Gerard Cochran, boasted that he personally 'would kill Joseph and scalp him and wear his scalp as a bridle'. On 9th

September, Joseph led seventy painted warriors to Cochran's cabin, and holding a war-club over him, asked to hear the boast again. Other settlers intervened, insisting that Cochran would leave the Wallowa immediately; and Joseph rode away peacefully.

With a militia from Grande Ronde mustering, Lieutenant Forse arrived with a troop from Fort Walla Walla on 10th September. Approaching Wallowa Lake, he found the Nez Perce warriors mounted on an impregnable high bluff, and reported: 'Joseph could have fallen upon the settlers in detail, killing them and destroying their property. . . . An enemy could not approach him without being under his fire for the distance of more than a half-mile.'

Upon receiving Forse's promise that the murderers would be arrested, Joseph agreed to keep his warriors in the vicinity of Wallowa Lake.

Although Findley was charged with manslaughter four days later, McNall, who the Nez Perce held responsible, was not. The Indians refused to testify at Findley's trial, and he was freed.

The Last Councils

Summoned to meet another commission, Joseph and Ollokot led a delegation up the Snake River in November 1876. On 13th November, the Wallowa delegation entered the Lapwai mission church, already crowded with Nez Perce, to meet the commissioners. Joining General Howard and Major Wood were three easterners, described by Monteith's wife as, 'kings of finance but with not a speck of Indian sense, experience or knowledge'. Though Howard believed himself to be championing Joseph's cause, his solution to the problem was simply to compensate the Wellamotkin band for its removal to Lapwai. The bible-thumping 'Christian General' dismissed Joseph's intrinsic love for his land as a reflection of his 'pagan' Dreamer religion.

For two days, Joseph rejected the commissioners' overtures to buy his territory, explaining simply: 'We love the land. It is our home'. As Joseph led his people away to winter in the Imnaha canyons, however, all the commissioners except Wood signed a report recommending the suppression of all Dreamer shamans, military occupation of the Wallowa and removal 'by force' of all non-treaty bands.

Instructed on 6th January 1877 to bring the Nez Perce on to the reservation within 'a reasonable time', Monteith set an over-eager deadline of 1st April. He foolishly declared, 'They can come one time just as well as another, having nothing to hinder them in moving'. Monteith then dispatched a group of treaty Nez Perce to deliver the ultimatum, to which Joseph responded:

I have been talking to the whites many years about the lands in question, and it is strange they cannot understand me; the country they claim belonged to my father, and when he died it was given to me and my people, and I will not leave it until I am compelled to.

Joseph was alarmed by Monteith's message, and bewildered that he could have been so misunderstood at the previous council. Through the Cayuse headman, Young Chief, he arranged another meeting with Howard, at the Umatilla Agency on 1st April – Monteith's optimistic deadline. Joseph fell seriously ill at this time, and so Ollokot, accompanied by a few Wellamotkin warriors and an elderly holy man, represented the Wallowa band. Ollokot had expected to meet Howard and receive his permission to settle on the Umatilla Agency rather than Lapwai. Instead, he was confronted by Howard's aide-de-camp Lieutenant Boyle, who sharply refuted the suggestion. Stretching out his arm, and spreading his fingers like a snake's tongue, Ollokot asked:

Nessameiek (liar), who are you? Where is General Howard? . . . I came a chief to talk to a chief. General Howard sends one of his boys to give orders to the Nez Perce!   General Howard talks with a forked tongue! He has lied to the Nez Perce. Was he ashamed to meet men to whom he talked two ways? . . . He has insulted me! Made me ashamed before my people!

Old-time Nez Perce shirt of the 1840s, short in length and fashioned according to the shape of the animal skin. It is decorated with pierced holes – a feature common on Blackfoot Indian shirts and possibly invoking sacred protection against bullets – and with the uncommon technique of wrapping horsehair in porcupine quills.

The council dissolved in ill humour, but on 20th April, Ollokot met Howard at Walla Walla. Howard re-iterated his demands for the Nez Perce to settle at Lapwai, but said that they would be given hunting and fishing passes for the Imnaha valley. A final council was arranged for Lapwai twelve days later, and Ollokot returned to his sick brother at a camp near Asotin, saying: 'Government wants all Indians put in one place. If you say "Yes" I will bring in the stock and we will go there. If the white officers ask what you will do, you answer, "Nothing to talk about, Ollokot has settled everything".'

Joseph's path, though, was not to be taken for him, and he prepared to travel to Lapwai.

On 4th May 1877, the council convened in a Lapwai hospital tent, and Howard was confronted by the anti-treaty headmen. Looking Glass, a formidable warrior of forty-five winters, was still talking against war. White Bird, the septuagenarian Salmon River warrior and chief, was described by Howard as, 'A demure looking Indian . . . . His face assumed the condition of . . . rigid fixedness while in council . . . ; he kept his immense ceremonial hat on, and placed a large eagle's wing in front of his eyes and nose'.

The Nez Perce elected Toohoolhoolzote as their spokesman, the eloquent, uncompromising Dreamer Shaman who could reputedly carry a slain deer on each shoulder. Howard called him a 'cross-grained growler', and a 'large thick-necked, ugly, obstinate savage of the worst type'.

Of Joseph and Ollokot, the general noted differently that they:

presented the finest appearance of the invited chiefs. Alokut (*sic*), the younger of the two, was even taller than his brother, as graceful and supple as a cougar. Carefree and full of youthful enthusiasm, his happy disposition attracted whites and Indians alike. Clearly, he was the idol and leader of the young men.

Howard and Monteith argued their case against Toohoolhoolzote until the council was adjourned. As night fell, Howard ordered troops up to

Grande Ronde, Lewiston and Fort Walla Walla. When the two sides re-convened on 7th May, the non-treaty ranks had been swelled by the arrival of the Palouse under Hahtalekin and Husishusis Kute (Little Baldhead or Preacher), described by Howard as 'bright-eyed and oily', whose 'manner of extreme cunning inspired distrust'. Joseph arrived in sullen mood, having learnt that soldiers were marching through the Wallowa among his women and children. He confronted Howard:

The measure of the land and the measure of our bodies are the same. Say to us if you can say it, that you were sent by the Creative Power to talk to us. Perhaps you think the Creator sent you here to dispose of us as you see fit.

If I thought you were sent by the Creator I might be induced to think you had a right to dispose of me. Do not misunderstand me, but understand me fully with reference to my affection for the land. I never said that land was mine to do as I chose. The one who has a right to dispose of it is the one who has created it. I claim a right to live on my land, and accord you the privilege to live on yours.

To Howard's stubborn insistence that the Nez Perce move immediately to the reservation, Toohoolhoolzote answered: 'The earth is part of our body, and we never gave up the earth'. Howard replied, 'We do not wish to interfere with your religion, but you must talk about practicable things. Twenty times over you repeat that the earth is your mother, and about chieftainship of the earth. Let us hear it no more.'

Arguing from vastly different viewpoints, compromise proved impossible, until Toohoolhoolzote mumbled: 'What person pretends to divide the land and put me on it?'

Losing his temper, Howard roared, 'I am that man. I stand here for the President, and there is no spirit good or bad who will hinder me. My orders are plain and will be executed.'

The argument continued until Howard seized Toohoolhoolzote by the arm and marched him to the guardhouse, where he was locked away. 'If you do not mind me', the Christian General told the astonished headman, 'I will take my soldiers and drive you on the reservation!'

With Toohoolhoolzote imprisoned, soldiers marching among their families, and Howard bellowing threats, the Nez Perce chiefs acquiesced. With heads bowed they agreed to tour the reservation, but Yellow Wolf recalled: 'In peace councils force must not be talked. It was the same as showing us the rifle . . . . That was not suited for the Indians. That was what brought war, the arrest of this chief, and showing us the rifle.'

A week later, Howard released Toohoolhoolzote. Many years later, Joseph recalled Howard's words:

He informed us in a haughty spirit that he would give my people thirty days to go back home, collect all their stock, and move to the reservation, saying, 'If you are not here in that time, I shall consider that you want to fight, and will send my soldiers to drive you on'.

Joseph protested that he could not be ready to move in thirty days. His stock was scattered and the Snake River was very high. 'Let us wait until fall,' he asked Howard.

The one-armed general remained insistent though, supporting Monteith's opinion that if Joseph be 'allowed to have his own way at this time, it will only make him more stubborn in the future'.

Nez Perce gun case and saddle bag of about 1850. The buffalo and elk hide are decorated with red cloth and beads, sewn with a sinew.

Showing the Rifle

Joseph and Ollokot returned to their people on Joseph Creek, accompanied by Toohoolhoolzote. The shaman was still determined to resist and encouraged the growing unrest among the warriors. But Joseph was now resigned to moving to the reservation, saying: 'It required a strong heart to stand up against such talk, but I urged my people to be quiet, and not to begin a war.'

With unaccustomed haste, the Nez Perce herded up their scattered horses and cattle and at the end of May Joseph led his band and 6000 animals up the Imnaha valley. For two days they battled to cross the Snake River, swollen by winter's melted snows. The men, stripped to breech-cloths, plunged into the torrential waters on horseback, and hauled the women and children across on great buffalo-robe bundles filled with their belongings. Then the bellowing animals were driven into the torrent. Several hundred were swept downstream, and the settlers eagerly claimed those animals that refused to attempt the crossing.

Miraculously, the Nez Perce emerged without loss of life, and proceeded wearily and bitterly up Rocky Canyon. Leaving their cattle west of the Salmon, they crossed the river to join the other non-treaty bands at Tepahlewam. Here, 600 Nez Perce enjoyed their last days of freedom, digging the bountiful camas, dancing, gambling and racing their horses.

Battle of White Bird Canyon

After a week, Joseph, his daughter Hophoponmi (Sound of Running Feet), Ollokot, his wife Wetatonmi, and the half-man, half-woman Welweyas re-crossed the Salmon to butcher beef. Returning to camp several days later with twelve horses laden with meat, they were met by a warrior named Two Moons, who announced that the war had started.

In Joseph's absence, one of White Bird's young men, Wahlitits (Shore Crossing) – whose father, Eagle Robe, had been murdered by settlers two winters before – had trampled some drying kouse roots during a horseback parade. Yellow Grizzly Bear had rebuked him: 'Playing brave, you ride over my woman's hard-worked food! If you are so brave, why not go kill the white man who killed your father?'

Wahlitits, with his cousin Sarpsis Ilppilp (Red Moccasin Tops) and

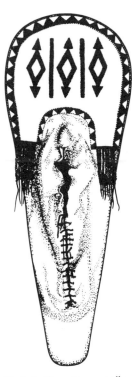

Typical Nez Perce cradle-board, with buckskin-covered wooden board and geometric beadwork decoration (above). Comparison (below) of Nez Perce (left) and Crow (right) cradleboard designs, the shaded areas indicating the beaded or decorated areas.

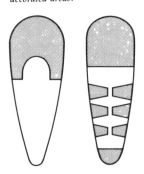

nephew Swan Necklace, had set out to do just that. Unable to locate his father's murderers, he killed four other Salmon River settlers against whom the Nez Perce nursed particular grievances.

Joseph galloped into Tepahlewam to find the Indians fleeing. He urged them to stay, in the forlorn hope of restoring peace; but soon only his own followers' lodges remained. The other bands whispered that Joseph would now head for Lapwai, abandoning them as Lawyer had done.

The Wallowa headman remained at Tepahlewam through the night, and in this time of killing, his wife gave birth to their second daughter. In the morning, Joseph led his people sixteen miles to White Bird Creek, and into the war he had tried so hard to avoid. He joined Toohoolhlzote and White Bird, whose warriors had by now killed fourteen settlers on Salmon River. Looking Glass remained at peace, having returned to his village at Kooskia.

On 15th June, Howard sent 92 cavalrymen from Fort Lapwai under Captain Perry to pursue the Nez Perce, teasing his subordinate: 'You must not get whipped'. To this, Perry replied: 'There is no danger of that, sir'.

On 15th June 1877, a scout's coyote howl alerted the Nez Perce camp in White Bird Canyon to Perry's approach. His command had travelled seventy miles in thirty hours, and had been reinforced en route by eleven settlers under Arthur Chapman. At dawn, a six-man truce party under Vicious Weasel (Wettiwetti Howlis) rode forward with a white flag. Approaching the canyon's sloping mouth, the delegation met Perry's advance detachment under Lieutenant Theller. As Vicious Weasel cried, 'What do you people want?' Chapman opened fire. An old Nez Perce warrior named Fire Body responded, shooting Perry's lead bugler from his saddle.

As the soldiers deployed into a thin line across the canyon, sixteen warriors under Two Moons charged Chapman's volunteers on Perry's left. The civilians were routed, exposing the left flank of Theller's dismounted central line. Emerging from a concealing butte, Ollokot, wearing a sash and riding a magnificent cream-coloured mount, led fifty warriors in a frontal assault against Theller. On Ollokot's left, Wahlitits, Red Moccasin Tops and Strong Eagle (Tipyahlahnah Kapskaps), all wearing red blanket coats to flaunt their bravery, broke the soldier line. With both flanks exposed, Theller's troops took to their heels, and 'the panic became general'. Hanging beneath their horse's bellies, Nez Perce warriors swept through the fleeing soldiers, and opened fire in their rear. Eighteen men under Lieutenant Theller were cut off and slain.

The warriors pursued Perry to within four miles of Mount Idaho, before returning to gather sixty-three rifles from the battleground. Only three Nez Perce were wounded in the encounter, and Joseph accurately recalled:

We numbered in that battle sixty men, and the soldiers a hundred. The fight lasted but a few minutes, when the soldiers retreated before us for twelve miles. They lost thirty-three killed and had seven wounded. When an Indian fights, he only shoots to kill; but soldiers shoot at random. None of the soldiers were scalped. We do not believe in scalping, nor in killing wounded men. Soldiers do not kill many Indians unless they are wounded. Then they kill Indians.

The following morning, the Nez Perce camp was further heartened by the return of the formidable warriors Five Wounds and Rainbow from buffalo-hunting in Montana. The headmen councilled, and on 19th June the Nez Perce re-crossed to the Salmon River's west bank. Thirty warriors remained behind as scouts.

The scouts flourished their red blankets to announce General Howard's approach several days later. Having left Fort Lapwai five days before with 227 regulars and 20 volunteers, Howard reached the Salmon at White Bird Canyon on 27th June having been reinforced en route to 400 soldiers plus 100 scouts and packers. The Nez Perce scouts taunted Howard from the far bank of the river. They were, according to Joseph, 'hoping General Howard would follow. We were not disappointed'

While Howard gingerly tested the Salmon's swirling waters, the Nez Perce, on 1st July, quietly packed camp and withdrew north-west into the pine-covered mountains. Toohoolhoolzote, Rainbow and Five Wounds led the warriors, while Joseph guided the women, children and elderly through the treacherous but familiar terrain. Thirty-six hours later, the cavalcade re-crossed the Salmon at Craig's Ferry some twenty five miles to the north. They camped at a kouse ground called Aipadass, west of Camas Prairie, having severed Howard's supply line.

Howard spent the entire day crossing the Salmon, before blundering after his elusive quarry. Battling up slippery trails and losing several pack-mules in precipitous canyons, Howard finally reached Craig's Ferry four days later. Commandeering and demolishing a house belonging to a treaty Nez Perce, Luke Billy, the soldiers constructed a raft; then watched the boat, its occupants and Luke Billy's home career downstream for four miles. Defeated, Howard doubled back into the tortuous mountains, re-traced his arduous journey, and re-crossed the Salmon at White Bird Canyon. Outwitted and outmanoeuvred, he reached Grangeville on 8th July.

Nez Perce bowcase, quiver and bandoleer of about 1870. The quiver and bowcase are made of buffalo hide covered with otter skins and adorned with beaded cuffs. From the top of the quiver and bowcase hang two elaborately decorated panels beaded in the style of the Crow, with pendants of fur and red cloth. The case and quiver were carried by means of the bandoleer which is decorated with red and dark blue stroud, otter fur and small triangles of beadwork. This excellent example was collected from a descendant of Ollokot.

Looking Glass

Having received misleading reports that Looking Glass was planning mischief, Howard had, on 29th June, dispatched two cavalry companies under Captain Whipple to arrest the chief. Breakfasting in his lodge two days later, Looking Glass was alerted to the approach of Whipple's troops, with twenty Mount Idaho civilians led by D.B. Randall. Bird Alighting (Peopeo Tholekt) rode out to parley, but returned in consternation after one of the civilians repeatedly jabbed a rifle into his ribs.

The Nez Perce raised a white flag, and Bird Alighting, accompanied by an old man named Kalowet, rode out again to tell the soldiers: 'Leave us alone. We are living here peacefully and want no trouble'. Whipple insisted upon seeing Looking Glass, and as Bird Alighting returned to his chief's lodge, a civilian suddenly shot a watching Nez Perce to the ground. The firing became general and as Looking Glass's people scattered, a woman and her baby were drowned trying to cross the Clearwater. After destroying the abandoned village's crops and rounding up the Nez Perce cattle, Whipple's troops marched north-west to Cottonwood, having 'stirred up a new hornet's nest'.

On the morning of 3rd July, Charles Blewell, a civilian scouting for Whipple, was killed by one of Joseph's scouts. He alerted the Nez Perce camp at Aipadass, whereupon Rainbow and Five Wounds led a war-party to attack Cottonwood. They came instead upon another of Whipple's scouting parties, under Lieutenant S.M. Rains, and wiped out the entire twelve-man detachment. The Nez Perce attacked Cottonwood the following day, but reinforcements from Lapwai, under Perry, helped resist the assault.

On 5th July, Joseph and the older fighters shepherded their people east across the Camas Prairie towards Piswah Ilppilp Pah (Place of Red Rock), guarded by an advance screen of fourteen warriors. These warriors stumbled upon seventeen civilian volunteers under Randall, heading for Cottonwood from Mount Idaho. The volunteers made a desperate charge through the Nez Perce ranks towards Perry's position but were forced to make a stand against the warriors' close pursuit. Besieged from 11.00 a.m. to mid-afternoon, Randall and another civilian were killed and three others wounded, before Perry belatedly dispatched a relief force. An aged warrior named Wounded Mouth (Mimpow Owyeen) was also killed.

Pausing only to bury Wounded Mouth, the Nez Perce bands travelled on to the south fork of the Clearwater. There their numbers were swelled to 200 fighting men and 500 elders, women and children by the arrival of Looking Glass, who declared bitterly: 'Now, my people, as long as I live I will never make peace with the treacherous Americans. I am ready for war.'

Leaving the War in Idaho

Nez Perce moccasins of the late nineteenth century and decorated with 'scatter-beading'. This type of decoration, consisting of individually stitched beads, was found only among a few of the Plateau tribes.

Four days after the fight with Randall, the Nez Perce's Clearwater camp was alerted, on 9th July, to the presence of eighty Lewiston volunteers under Colonel G. McConville, dug in on Possossona Hill. For two days, Ollokot, Five Wounds and Rainbow led frequent attacks against the soldiers' position, which became aptly known as Misery Hill, and forty-eight horses stolen by Whipple from Looking Glass's village were re-captured.

Since scouts had reported no signs of Howard's anticipated arrival from the south-west, the Nez Perce remained contentedly on the Clearwater. Their calm, though, was shattered by the sudden explosion of a howitzer shell in the early afternoon of 11th July. The one-armed General, reinforced by Perry, had led 400 regulars and 150 volunteers across the Clearwater south of Joseph's camp. Proceeding north along a plateau high above the eastern bank of the river, he had stumbled upon the Nez Perce.

While Howard attempted to organise his straggling, two-mile-long column into a cohesive attacking force, he came under fire from twenty-four snipers organised by Toohoolhoolzote. Warriors including Ollokot meanwhile scampered up the slope and mounted a defensive fire into the soldiers' flanks from improvised rifle-pits. Joseph divided his time between fighting and councilling with the other headmen in a concealed 'smoking lodge'.

As sporadic fighting continued through the next day, many Nez Perce warriors became keen to withdraw. In mid-afternoon, Joseph rode down from the lines to organise the packing of the lodges, but, Yellow Wolf recalled: 'The women, not knowing the warriors were disagreeing, quitting the fight, had no time to pack the camp. Chief Joseph did not reach them soon enough.' As Perry's cavalry advanced, the warriors retreated, and the women were forced to abandon their camp. Only Perry's hesitancy permitted the Nez Perce to withdraw safely north up the Clearwater to Kamiah. Lodges, clothing and large amounts of flour were lost to the soldiers, and war correspondent Tom Sutherland reported his discovery of 'a much worn pair of small moccasins and an absurd little rag doll under a tree'.

The Nez Perce lost four warriors – Going Across (Wayakot), Grizzly Bear Blanket (Yoomtis Kunnin), Red Thunder (Heinmot Ilppilp) and

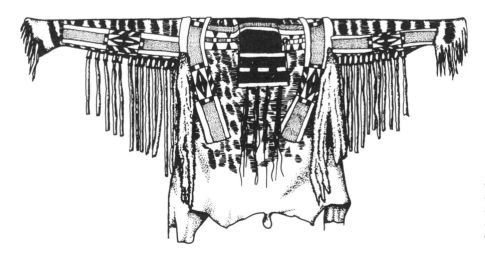

This war-shirt of around 1865 and accredited to Joseph, illustrates the close relationship between the costume of the Nez Perce and that of the Crow tribe of the Great Plains.

31

Whittling (Lelooskin) – while fifteen of Howard's troops were killed. Although the soldiers reported 'Joseph is in full flight', Howard foolishly delayed his pursuit until the sun rose the following day.

At dawn on 13th July, the Nez Perce scuttled across the Clearwater on their buffalo-bundle boats. As the last of their horses plunged across, Perry and Whipple's cavalry approached. They were scattered in panic by the Nez Perce warriors' fierce fire. According to Howard, the only damage inflicted, was, 'the shame to us and a fierce delight to the foe'.

'Plenty of Fighting'

The Nez Perce made camp on the Clearwater, which Howard dared not cross, then struck their lodges the following morning and headed for Weippe Prairie and the Lolo Trail east. A warrior named No Heart delayed the soldiers' pursuit, parleying across the river with Howard before promptly slapping his buttocks in derision and galloping away from the man the Nez Perce were now calling 'General Day After Tomorrow'.

At Weippe Prairie, the people's future was discussed by the headmen: Joseph, White Bird, Looking Glass, Toohoolhoolzote and Hahtalekin, who had recently brought sixteen Palouse warriors to join the cause. Joseph told them:

Some of you tried to say, once, that I was afraid of the whites. Stay here with me, and you shall have plenty of fighting. We will put our women behind us in the mountains, and die in our own land fighting for them. I would rather do that than run I know not where.

Looking Glass's voice, though, dominated the council, and it was agreed that he should lead the Nez Perce on the Lolo trail over the Bitterroots, to join the Crows in Montana, and perhaps on to the 'Old Woman's Country', Canada, where Sitting Bull had sought sanctuary after the Custer massacre. 'We intended to go peaceably to the buffalo country', Joseph noted, 'and leave the question of returning to our country to be settled afterward'.

Fort Fizzle

While the people followed the rugged Lolo Trail high into the mountains, to camp at Mussel Creek, five warriors left behind as scouts discovered Howard's advance party under Major E.C. Mason. The soldiers were being guided by treaty Nez Perce, who were ambushed on 17th July by Joseph's warriors. Scout John Levi's body was later found with forty-five bullet wounds, indicating the fugitive Nez Perces' anger toward their own people's treachery. Mason retreated to Howard on the Clearwater where the one-armed General idled for a fortnight, allowing the Nez Perce to trail out of his jurisdiction.

The tortuously narrow Lolo Trail, blocked by crags, trees and undergrowth, was quickly traversed by Joseph's uncomplaining cavalcade.

Caught in the horse-herd, Joseph rescues his daughter from advancing troopers of the 2nd Cavalry, after General Miles' attack in a snowy hollow of the Bear Paws Mountains, 8.00 a.m., 30th September 1877.

Howard later reported that the Nez Perce had 'jammed their ponies through, up the rocks . . . and among the fallen trees, without attempting to cut a limb, leaving blood to mark their path; and abandoned animals with broken legs . . . or stretched dead by the wayside.'

The Nez Perce then descended the eastern Bitterroots into Montana on 25th July to find their path blocked by a crude stockade, subsequently dubbed 'Fort Fizzle'. It was manned by thirty-five regulars under Captain C.C. Rawn summoned from Fort Missoula by Howard, plus 200 Montana volunteers and, to the Nez Perce's disgust, twenty Flathead Indians. Joseph, Looking Glass and White Bird calmly approached the defenders under a white flag. For three days they parleyed; Rawn demanding their surrender and the Nez Perce asking to be allowed into Montana in peace. 'We are going by you without fighting if you will let us', Joseph warned, 'but we are going by you anyhow'. Looking Glass chided Rawn: 'If the officer wishes to build corrals for the Nez Perce he may, but they will not hold us back. We are not horses.'

At 10.00 a.m. on 28th July, those of Rawn's men who hadn't by now deserted reported that they:

heard singing apparently above our heads. Upon looking up, we discovered the Indians passing along the side of the cliff, where we thought a goat could not pass, much less an entire tribe of Indians, with all their impedimenta. The entire band dropped into the valley beyond us, and then proceeded up the Bitterroot.

'No more fighting!' Yellow Wolf declared optimistically, 'We had left General Howard and his war in Idaho.'

Big Hole Battle

While the Nez Perce procession passed high above Fort Fizzle, a screening line of warriors exchanged shots briefly with the soldiers. Three civilian volunteers were captured, then quickly released with instructions to inform the Montana settlers of the Nez Perces' peaceful intentions.

Camping in the Bitterroot valley, the headmen councilled once more. Ignoring advice to head directly north to Canada, Looking Glass insisted upon travelling south to Crow country. Joseph complied, saying: 'I have no words. You know the country, I do not.'

For ten days the Nez Perce trailed slowly south, trading peacefully with settlements on the Bitterroot. Their caravan was joined by a small Nez Perce group resident in the valley, and by a half-blood called Lean Elk or Poker Joe. Looking Glass kept the warriors under close control, and offered horses as compensation when one of Toohoolhoolzote's followers stole some flour.

At the southern end of the valley, the band passed the revered

A blanket wrapped about him against the cold, his bravest warriors at his flanks, Joseph rides out to make peace with Generals Miles and Howard, and their officers, in the Bear Paws Mountains, 5th October 1877.

Medicine Tree, an ancient yellow pine in which a mountain sheep horn was embedded eight feet above the ground, considered a place of sanctuary and Wyakin powers. In subsequent camps, several men experienced visions of foreboding. Wahlitits prophesied his own death, and the warrior Lone Bird intoned: 'My shaking heart tells me trouble and death will overtake us if we make no hurry through this land!'

Looking Glass dismissed his people's fears and refused even to post scouts when the Nez Perce reached Iskumtselauk, Place of Ground Squirrels, by the Big Hole River, on 7th August. Pitching their eighty-nine lodges on the river's eastern bank, the people grazed their ponies in the westerly hills and cut new lodge poles which were to be dragged to the Crow country when seasoned.

At dawn on 9th August, Natalekin, a short-sighted old man, rode out towards the horse herds. Dimly making out figures, he leant forward on his mount, and a volley of fire tore him to the ground. A long line of soldiers splashed across the river and poured their fire into the silent lodges.

The soldiers, numbering 17 officers, 146 men, and 35 volunteers, were led by veteran Indian fighter Colonel John Gibbon, who had been wired by Howard on 25th July at Fort Shaw. They had approached the camp silently the previous night, while Howard, with 700 soldiers, emerged from an arduous crossing of the Lolo Trail.

Gibbon launched a three-pronged attack from the north, north-west and west, cutting the Indians down as they stumbled from their lodges. Some warriors desperately engaged the leading soldiers. Others fled among the riverside willows, and then circled around the soldiers' rear. The women and children rushed for the shelter of the riverbank. Rainbow, whose *Wyakin* served him only after sunrise, fell in the first attack when his rifle jammed. Five Wounds, in his grief, was killed making a lone charge. Captain Logan fulfilled Wahlitits' omen of death and then fell himself as Wahlitits' wife took up the warrior's rifle.

Joseph's lodge was at the north of the camp, and one of his wives was cut down by a bullet while carrying her daughter to safety. Joseph, bare-footed and wearing just a shirt and blanket, had led a charge across the river to rescue the horses. He returned to carry screaming children to safety, while White Bird and Looking Glass organised their warriors into sharp-shooting positions. 'Almost every time one of their rifles went off', Gibbon lamented, 'one of our party was sure to fall.'

After four hours of fighting, Gibbon, wounded in the thigh, ordered a retreat to a wooded plateau to the south-west. Digging in, the soldiers resisted a fierce onslaught from Ollokot's warriors. To the west, a group led by Bird Alighting seized Gibbon's pack-train, destroying a mountain howitzer and capturing 20,000 rounds of Springfield ammunition.

Joseph now urged his grieving people to strike their lodges. Gibbon had ordered his men to take no prisoners, and the Nez Perce women

were crying for the dead, the children screaming from their pain. Yellow Wolf told how he found one tipi containing two women shot dead, one still clasping her newborn baby with its head smashed as by a gun breech or boot heel. In another, he found two other children, both killed. 'Some soldiers acted with crazy minds,' he said later.

Despite possessing the advantage of numbers and surprise, Gibbon had lost twenty-nine men, including seven officers, and suffered forty wounded, two mortally. The Nez Perce reported the deaths of 'Fifty women and children and thirty fighting men', including such treasured warriors as Rainbow and Five Wounds. Leaving a dozen men under Ollokot to besiege Gibbon, Joseph led his people south at noon, hauling the wounded on travois and noting sadly: 'The Nez Perce never make war on women and children; we could have killed a great many women and children while the war lasted, but we would feel ashamed to do so cowardly an act.'

The Net Closes

The Nez Perce hurried south under the shadow of the Bitterroots, guided now by Poker Joe, since Looking Glass carried the burden of blame for the Big Hole disaster. Ollokot re-joined the camp at Lake Creek, where his wife Fair Land (Aihits Palojame) died from her wounds, leaving a baby named Tuekakas after its grandfather. Reaching Horse Prairie on 12th August, the chiefs could no longer restrain the warriors from killing five settlers in raids for fresh horses. At Junction, on the Lemhi River, the Nez Perce found the settlements fortified, and were warned off by Chief Tenday of the Lemhi Shoshoni. Heading south-east, some Nez Perce captured a wagon-train laden with whiskey, and in a drunken orgy killed five freighters and one of their own warriors, Kettalkpoosmin.

General Howard had meanwhile reached the Big Hole on 10th August and resumed his pursuit three days later, after watching his Bannock scouts mutilate the Nez Perce dead. On 17th August the Nez Perce camped at Beaver Creek. Howard, a day's march behind them, dispatched forty-three troopers under Lieutenant G. Bacon east to Targhee Pass to intercept the Nez Perce if they turned north for the Crow country.

Howard spent the night of 19th August at Camas Meadows, a few

U.S. army mountain howitzer and carriage, like that seized from General Gibbon by Peopeo Tholekt (Bird Alighting) at the Battle of the Big Hole.

miles south-east of the Nez Perce camp. Assured of success by the dream of a warrior called Black Hair, twenty-eight warriors, including Ollokot, Looking Glass, Toohoolhoolzote, Two Moons and Bird Alighting, stealthily entered Howard's camp at 3.30 a.m. to steal his horses. However, the premature report of one warrior's gun alerted the soldiers, and the raiders hurriedly stampeded 200 mules. Three cavalry companies gave pursuit, but were scattered when the warriors turned to defend a lava escarpment. Three soldiers were killed and six wounded, delaying Howard's pursuit for another day.

On 22nd August, the Nez Perce cavalcade trailed through Targhee Pass, recently vacated by Lieutenant Bacon in the belief that the Indians had already eluded him. Proceeding up Madison River, the fugitives entered what in 1872 had become Yellowstone National Park, and were guided east by a captured prospector, John Shively. Some warriors also seized nine bewildered tourists, wounding two of them before the chiefs interceded. One captive described Joseph as 'Sombre and silent, foreseeing in his gloomy meditations possibly the unhappy ending of his campaign . . . . Grave and dignified, he looked a chief.'

Joseph had reason for his concern, for Commanding General Sherman, currently visiting the park, had intensified his military campaign. To the north of Joseph, two companies of cavalry and one of Crow scouts waited at Mammoth Hot Springs; General George Crook had deployed five cavalry companies on Shoshoni River and ten 5th Cavalry companies on Wind River to the east and south-east respectively; Colonel Nelson 'Bearcoat' Miles lurked at Fort Keogh; and in the north-east Colonel S.D. Sturgis' six 7th Cavalry companies, accompanied by Crow scouts, waited on Clark's Fork. The *New North-west* reported:

General Sherman . . . has raised up an army on the four sides of Joseph just when it seemed most probable that he was about to escape. . . . We wait now hopefully for news that the Nez Perces have been struck hard and fatally.

As Poker Joe guided the people north-east, the warriors killed several white men attempting to carry messages between the soldiers. When they sighted Sturgis' command on 8th September, the Nez Perce suddenly turned south. Believing Clark's Fork Canyon to be impassable, and convinced that Joseph was escaping, Sturgis set off in pursuit. Out of sight, the Nez Perces milled their ponies to confuse their trail, then doubled north once more, concealed by the timbered mountain slopes. Passing close to, and parallel with, Sturgis' southbound command, the Nez Perce band silently traversed the now unguarded Clark's Fork Canyon, 'where rocks on either side came so near together that two horses abreast could hardly pass'. They emerged north of the Absaroke Mountains, having brilliantly outfoxed their pursuers once more. Sturgis re-entered Clark's Fork in Howard's rear on 11th September, much to the general's chagrin. Reaching the junction of the Yellowstone and Canyon Creek, Looking Glass rode ahead to council with the Crow chiefs on whom he had relied so heavily. He returned with his head bowed, saying that the Crows, his closest friends, would offer no help.

Death in the Bear Paws

On 13th September, the Nez Perce scouts flourished their red blankets to warn of the approach of Sturgis, who had marched sixty miles the previous day. As the warriors turned to fight, Joseph hurried the helpless ones towards the gorge into which Canyon Creek ran. Ollokot overtook them and joined a group of warriors in resisting Captain Benteen's attempt to outflank the fleeing families. As Sturgis frustrated his own attack by ordering his troopers to dismount, the Nez Perce secured the mouth of the narrow canyon. The band retreated safely, blocking pursuit with rocks and fallen trees.

Hastening north towards the Musselshell River early the next morning, the Nez Perce fought a fierce rearguard action against Sturgis' Bannock and Crow scouts which continued for two days and resulted in the deaths of one Nez Perce warrior and two old men, and the capture of forty horses. Sturgis suffered three dead and eleven wounded.

The Nez Perce crossed the Musselshell on 17th September and raided fresh horses from Crow chief Dumb Bull's camp. Crossing the Judith Mountains, Poker Joe set a hard pace, and the elderly and wounded silently drifted behind their people. The Nez Perce reached the Missouri on 23rd September, where they asked to trade with the fifteen soldiers at Cow Island Landing supply station. Insulted by Commander Moelchert's offer of a side of bacon and half a sack of hardtack, the warriors looted the station for flour, sugar, coffee, pots and pans. One of the soldiers wired Fort Benton:

The array of rifles employed by the Nez Perce on the Camas Meadows battlefield.

Chief Joseph is here, and says he will surrender for two hundred bags of sugar. I told him to surrender without the sugar. He took the sugar and will not surrender. What will I do?

Pushing north the following day, the Nez Perce looted a wagon-train, killing three teamsters, and skirmished briefly with soldiers from Fort Benton. Weary of the hurried march, the chiefs again placed themselves under Looking Glass's protection, though Poker Joe warned: 'All right, Looking Glass, you can lead. I am trying to save the people, doing my best to cross over into Canada before the soldiers find us. You can take command, but I think we will be caught and killed.'

For four days, Looking Glass led the band lazily north, and Joseph noted: 'We had heard nothing of General Howard, or Gibbon, or Sturgis. We had repulsed each in turn, and began to feel secure.' After visiting with Assiniboin Indians, the Nez Perce camped in the ravines on the east bank of Snake Creek between the Bear Paw Mountains and the Milk River. In a depression sheltered from the snow-laden winds, but open to attack on three sides, it was a good place to rest, but a poor place to fight. Toohoolhoolzote camped to the north, Looking Glass, White Bird, Husishusis Kute and Koolkool Snehee in the centre, and Joseph, Ollokot and Poker Joe to the south. The warrior Wottolen protested in vain to Looking Glass that he had seen a vision of disaster at this place.

At sunrise on 30th September, stampeding buffalo alerted the camp to approaching soldiers. As the women struck the lodges, a Nez Perce scout signalled: 'Enemies right on us! Soon the attack!' At 8.00 a.m. 383 men under General Miles – having made four days of forced marches from Fort Keogh – swarmed over the southern bluffs. The camp was thrown into turmoil, with warriors sprinting to natural rifle-pits, and the helpless ones taking flight north. Joseph's voice rose above the uproar, barking, 'Horses! Horses! Save the horses!', as the chief splashed across the creek to gather mounts for the fleeing families.

Miles attacked in two sweeping wings from south and east, the 7th Cavalry striking the south with their commander Captain Hale complaining, 'My God, have I got to go out and get killed in such cold weather!' The Nez Perce marksmen met his cavalry charge with a withering volley, reducing it to a bloody mêlée of screaming men and horses. Twenty-four soldiers, including Hale, fell dead, with forty-two wounded; and Lieutenant Erickson wheeled around to scream at Miles, 'I am the only damned man of the Seventh Cavalry who wears shoulder straps alive!'

Captain Tyler's 2nd Cavalry, with some Cheyenne scouts, circled west into the Nez Perce horse herd, separating Joseph and his warriors from the main camp.

We had no knowledge of General Miles' army until a short time before he made a charge upon us, cutting our camp in two, and capturing nearly all of the horses. About seventy men, myself among them, were cut off. My little daughter, twelve years of age, was with me. I gave her a rope, and told her to catch a horse and join the others who were cut off from the camp.

(Joseph)

Startled by the camp's ferocious defence, Miles mustered the 5th Infantry for a charge 'towards the village on foot, but the withering fire of the Indians soon proved too severe, and attempts to capture the village by such means had to be abandoned.' Reluctantly, Miles formed his men into a thin line around the village, and the assault degenerated into a siege.

In a fresh attack in the afternoon, the bluecoats penetrated the camp from the south-west:

The soldiers kept up a continuous fire. Six of my men were killed in one spot near me. Ten or twelve soldiers charged into our camp and got possession of two lodges, killing three Nez Perce and losing three of their men, who fell inside our lines. I called my men to drive them back. We fought at close range, not more than twenty steps apart, and drove the soldiers back upon their main lines, leaving their dead in our hands. We secured their ammunition. We lost, the first day and night, eighteen men and three women.

(Joseph)

Four of those killed, including Poker Joe, had been mistakenly shot by their own warriors. Toohoolhoolzote and Hahtelekin also lay dead, but the sadness in Joseph's heart was for Ollokot, who had tragically fallen in the thick of the early fighting.

The Boston Truce

Five inches of snow fell through the night. A woman of the band later recalled how the besieged Nez Perce dug shelter-pits for the helpless ones and rifle-pits for the warriors:

We digged the trenches with camas hooks and butcher knives. With pans we threw out the dirt . . . . Dried meat would be handed round. If not enough for all, it would be given to the children first. I was three days without food. Children cried with hunger and cold. Old people suffering in silence. Misery everywhere. Cold and dampness all around.

Six warriors escaped north to seek help from the 2000 Lakota living in Canada under Sitting Bull, but they were murdered by the same Assiniboin Indians who had been their hosts two days before.

When the report of Miles' Hotchkiss gun heralded morning, the Nez Perce were entrenched in a remarkable network of tunnels. The fighting was at stalemate until noon, when the soldiers raised a white flag, and a voice cried out in the Chinook jargon: 'Colonel Miles would like to see Chief Joseph'. The chiefs hurriedly councilled, and Joseph, less intransigent than some of the headmen, agreed to meet Miles. After sending a half-blood, Tom Hill, to arrange the parley, Joseph rode out with two warriors. Miles met them, and clasping Joseph's hand, said, 'Come; let us sit down by the fire and talk this matter over'.

This Nez Perce knife and sheath date from the late nineteenth century and are decorated with beadwork in designs that continue to demonstrate a strong Plains influence.

The parley was unproductive, with Miles demanding unconditional surrender of all arms and Joseph requesting that his people be allowed to return peaceably to the Wallowa, while retaining half their guns for hunting. In his frustration, Miles led Joseph back to his command tent, where, in flagrant violation of the flag of truce, he took the stoic chief prisoner. 'That', Lieutenant Jerome stated, 'was Miles' way'.

Fortunately for Joseph, Jerome misread the situation and rode into the Indian camp, where he himself was seized. Held through the night, he wrote the following morning: 'I am treated like I was at home. I hope you officers are treating Chief Joseph as I am treated.' According to Yellow Wolf, though, 'Joseph was bound hands and feet. They took a double blanket . . . rolled him in it like you roll a papoose on a cradle board . . . put where there were mules, not in soldier tent.'

When Yellow Bull visited his detained chief, Joseph told him, 'I do not know what they mean to do with me, but if they kill me, you must not kill the officer. It will do no good to avenge my death by killing him.' That afternoon, though, the two hostages were escorted to a buffalo robe spread between the lines, where, shaking hands, they were exchanged.

Sporadic firing and the misery of Joseph's people continued for the next two days. On 4th October, Miles' Napoleon cannon, raised like a mortar, inflicted the first Indian casualties since the opening battle: burying a girl, Atsipeeten, and her grandmother, Intetah, in their shelter. The people were divided about surrendering, and White Bird deferred to Joseph's judgement. The chief's despair was completed by the arrival that evening of General Howard with the vanguard of his army.

Towards noon on 5th October, Howard's treaty Nez Perce scouts Captain John and Old George carried a white flag to the fugitives' lines and asked them to make peace. Sending the messengers 'back where they belonged', Joseph consulted Looking Glass and White Bird. They both refused to surrender to a 'man of two faces', but Joseph said, 'Many of our people are out on the hills, naked and freezing. The women are suffering with cold, the children crying with the chilling dampness of the shelter pits. For myself I do not care. It is for them I am going to surrender.'

When Captain John and Old George returned to say that Miles wished to have no more war, and would return the Nez Perce to the reservation, Joseph became convinced that he was now being asked to negotiate not a surrender, but a peace.

As a tragic postscript, a mounted Indian approached the battleground that afternoon. Believing him to be one of Sitting Bull's warriors, Looking Glass leapt from his rifle-pit. The horseman was, in fact, one of Miles' Cheyenne scouts, and Looking Glass was cut down by a sharp-shooter's bullet; the only warrior to die after the opening battle.

'From Where the Sun Now Stands'

In a preliminary council, Joseph received Miles' assurance that his people could winter with Miles on the Yellowstone before returning to Lapwai. The Nez Perce were confident of a return to their homeland. 'Everybody', according to Howard's adjutant Lieutenant Wood, 'took this as an accepted fact'.

At 2.00 p.m. Joseph rode slowly from the southern end of the camp, with five warriors walking beside him and leaning against his horse's flanks. Joseph was shrouded beneath a grey, black-striped blanket, and rested his rifle across his saddle pommel. Bullets had scarred his wrists and forehead, and torn his shirt and leggings. The silent contingent approached a buffalo robe laid between the lines where Miles, Howard, Wood, two more officers, interpreter Arthur Chapman, an orderly and a mounted courier waited.

Dismounting, Joseph drew his blanket around him and, carrying his rifle in the crook of his arm, proudly offered it to Howard. The general deferred this honour to Miles, before Joseph stepped back to deliver his speech of surrender:

Tell General Howard I know his heart. What he told me before, I have in my heart, I am tired of fighting. Our chiefs are killed. Looking Glass is dead. Toohoolhoolzote is dead. The old men are all killed. It is the young men who say yes or no. He who led the young men[Ollokot] is dead.

An unusual photograph of Joseph presented to the U.S. National Archives by General Miles. Joseph wears a blanket, leggings and war-shirt with ermine drops. His hair is in braids, with a striking example of the raised Crow-style fringe characteristic of Joseph's band of the Nez Perce.

It is cold and we have no blankets. The little children are freezing to death. I want time to look for my children, and see how many of them I can find. Maybe I shall find them among the dead. Hear me, my chiefs. I am tired; my heart is sick and sad. From where the sun now stands, I will fight no more forever.

Then Joseph hid his head beneath his blanket, and with it the war.

Into Exile

The fight was the most fierce of any Indian engagement I have ever been in. . . . The whole Nez Perce movement is unequalled in the history of Indian warfare.

Such was Miles' view of the Nez Perces' epic struggle. They travelled 1,700 miles in eleven weeks, defied ten separate US commands, and capitulated only forty miles from the Canadian border. Of the 750 Nez Perce that had left Idaho, 120 had died, and 87 men, 184 women and 147 children surrendered under Joseph, with 1500 horses and 300 saddles; 180 whites had been killed in the campaign, with 150 wounded.

Joseph had been the guardian of the women and children throughout the long march, and though he conferred constantly with the other headmen, the whites regarded him as the figurehead of the Nez Perce resistance. After the surrender, reporter J.J. Healey wrote that Joseph was 'walking round about his people talking to the wounded and occasionally addressing the warriors by signs, and seemed quite unconcerned about his defeat.'

While most of the Nez Perce surrendered with Joseph, White Bird, with fourteen warriors and a similar number of women, escaped during the night. Yellow Wolf slipped away during a snowstorm the following morning, after Joseph had told him, 'You better go find your mother and my daughter. Bring them here!'

Joseph's 'old wife', Heyoom Yoyish (Bear Crossing) and daughter had fled during the opening battle, and were among some 230 Nez Perce who escaped from the Bear Paws to Sitting Bull's camp in Canada. From spring 1878 onwards, several small groups of these homesick exiles straggled back to the Lapwai Reservation.

On 8th October, Miles started his ragged caravan of troops and captives towards Fort Keogh, on the Tongue River. He arrived a week later, having developed a profound respect for the eloquent Joseph and his kinsmen. Commanding General Sherman, though, declared that the Nez Perce's confinement at the fort would prove too expensive. He instructed Miles instead to break his surrender terms, and herd the 432 prisoners 800 miles to Fort Lincoln, near Bismarck, North Dakota. Bearcoat complied reluctantly, ferrying the wounded up the Yellowstone and Missouri, and protesting the Nez Perce 'treatment unusually severe. Joseph can tell you his own story'.

In Bismarck, on 16th November, the ragged Nez Perce were received as heroes, reflecting the growing public sympathy for their plight. They received food in the town square while a band played the Star Spangled Banner, and Joseph received an invitation to a feast in his honour:

To Joseph, Head Chief of the Nez Perces. Sir: Desiring to show you our kind feeling and the admiration we have for your bravery and humanity, as exhibited in your recent conflict with the forces of the United States.

Amid the accolades, Joseph learnt that his people were to be sent as prisoners of war, by train, to Fort Leavenworth, eastern Kansas. He asked: 'When will the white man learn to tell the truth?'

Eeikish Pah – The Hot Place

On 27th November 1877, Joseph's people disembarked at Fort Leavenworth. They were ordered to camp in a swampy depression beside the Missouri which one observer suggested had been selected 'for the express purpose of putting an end to Chief Joseph and his band'. Malaria was rife and by the following July it had claimed twenty one Nez Perce lives.

We had always lived in a healthy country, where the mountains were high and the water was cold and clear. Many of our people sickened and died, and we buried them in this strange land. I can not tell how much my heart suffered for my people while at Leavenworth. The Great Spirit . . . seemed to be looking some other way, and did not see what was being done to my people.

(Joseph)

A petition for a new home, submitted by Joseph in December 1877 and endorsed by Captain Randall at Fort Leavenworth, was disapproved by Sherman. In July 1878, though, the Bureau of Indian Affairs assumed responsibility for the Nez Perce, and transferred them south to the parched 7000-acre Quapaw Reservation in Kansas Territory. 'We were not asked if we were willing to go', Joseph recalled, 'We were ordered to get into the railroad cars. Three of my people died on the way'.

By October 1878, forty-seven more Nez Perce had died, in the land they hatefully called Eeikish Pah, The Hot Place. 'I think very little of this country', Joseph lamented, 'It is like a poor man; it amounts to nothing'. That month, Joseph's frequent complaints resulted in visits from Indian Commissioner E.A. Hayt and a congressional committee. Both parties concurred with the chief's protests, and Hayt accompanied Joseph and Husishusis Kute on a 250-mile tour of the southern plains. They selected a 90,710-acre area of the Ponca Reservation, Oklahoma as a possible new home for the Nez Perce, though it was little better.

When informed that his dream of a return to Idaho was out of the question, Joseph said:

This talk fell like a heavy stone upon my heart . . . . Other law chiefs came to see us and said they would help me to get a healthy country. I did not know who to believe. The

A Nez Perce dress from about 1890. It is made from two bighorn or deer skins decorated with paint and beadwork, the untrimmed tails ornamenting the middle of the bodice. Even in exile, the traditional crafts survived.

white people have too many chiefs. They do not understand each other. They do not talk alike.

Pleas in Vain

Through the efforts of Indian Inspector General John O'Neill, Joseph was granted permission to visit Washington with Yellow Bull and veteran interpreter Arthur Chapman, to meet President Hayes. On 14th January 1879, the 38-year-old chief stirred an important Lincoln Hall audience with a moving address:

I have shaken hands with a great many friends, but there are some things I want to know which no-one seems able to explain. I can not understand how the Government sends a man out to fight us, as it did General Miles, and then breaks his word. Such a Government has something wrong about it. I can not understand why so many chiefs are allowed to talk so many different ways, and promise so many different things. . . .

I have heard talk and talk, but nothing is done. Good words do not last long until they amount to something. . . . Good words will not give me back my children. . . . Good words will not give my people good health and stop them from dying. Good words will not get my people a home where they can live in peace, and take care of themselves. I am tired of talk that comes to nothing. It makes my heart sick when I remember all the good words and all the broken promises. . . .

If the white man wants to live in peace with the Indian he can live in peace. There need be no trouble. Treat all men alike. Give them all an even chance to live and grow. . . . The earth is mother of all people, and all people should have equal rights upon it. You

Chief Joseph, wearing an embroidered cotton shirt and beaded sash. It is likely that he was photographed in 1887, shortly after the Nez Perce war, probably at Bismark.

might as well expect the rivers to run backward as that any man who was born a free man should be contented penned up and denied liberty to go where he pleases. . . .

I only ask of the Government to be treated as all other men are treated. If I can not go to my own home, let me have a home in some country where my people will not die so fast. I would like to go to Bitter Root Valley. There my people would be healthy. . . .

Let me be a free man – free to travel, free to stop, free to work, free to trade where I choose, free to choose my own teachers, free to follow the religion of my fathers, free to think and talk and act for myself – and I will obey every law or submit to the penalty. . . .

I have asked some of the great white chiefs where they get their authority to say to the Indian that he shall stay in one place, while he sees white men going where they please. They can not tell me.

Joseph's words fell on stony ground. In June 1879, Hayt compromised by transferring Joseph's 370 Nez Perce about 180 miles west to Oakland on the Ponca Reservation. The Lapwai Nez Perce opened a school there, but the children continued to die. A visiting doctor counted the graves of 100 infants including the daughter born to Joseph on the eve of the Nez Perce flight at Tepahlewam.

In July 1879, Joseph despairingly told a group of white visitors:

You come to see me as you would a man upon his death-bed. The Great Spirit above has left me and my people to their fate. The white men forget us and death comes almost every day for some of my people. He will come for all of us. A few months more, and we will be in the ground. We are a doomed people.

The Final Heartbreak

Joseph's cause was adopted by General Miles, by the Presbyterian Church, and by the Indian Rights Association, and became a national issue. In May 1883, the school of Oakland closed, and twenty-nine widows and orphans were permitted to accompany teacher James Reuben back to Lapwai. A year later, the arrival of fourteen petitions persuaded Congress to give Secretary of the Interior H.M. Teller discretion in the matter.

Teller decided to return the White Bird and Looking Glass bands to Lapwai, but directed that Joseph's people should go to the Colville Reservation, north-east Washington, because the Idaho settlers still nursed grievances towards them. To this, Joseph protested: 'If I could, I would take my heart out and hold it in my hand and let the Great Father and the white people see that there is nothing in it but kind feelings and love for him and them.'

On 1st June 1885, a group comprising 118 of the exiled Nez Perce arrived at Lapwai, while Joseph's 150 followers continued on to the Colville Reservation. Even here, troops were required to settle the band peaceably, amid opposition from Agent Gwydir, the resident Sans Poil Indian chief Skolaskin and suspicious white traders. In December, the band migrated fifty miles west to the more productive Nespelem valley.

Distinctive Nez Perce 'corn-husk' bags of the late nineteenth century. They were woven from hemp and embroidered with wool.

In 1889, all the members of the Nez Perce tribe were offered allotments of 160 acres on the Lapwai Reservation; the surplus to be sold to the highest bidder. Joseph visited the Allotting Agent, but refused, on principle, to take any land other than the Wallowa valley. One observer noted, 'It was good to see an unsubjugated Indian. One could not help respecting the man who still stood firmly for his rights, after having fought and suffered and been defeated in the struggle for their maintenance.'

Joseph visited Lapwai with increasing frequency, and even participated in the old-time procession of warriors at the raucous 4th July celebrations. Missionary Kate McBeth wrote: 'For a few years at first Joseph was afraid to come down upon the Nez Perce reserve – afraid of the surrounding whites and because of the many indictments against him – but this fear wore off. Then he visited his friends – too often for their good for he held to his heathenism with all the tenacity with which he had clung to his beloved Wallowa Valley.'

When white squatters again threatened his lands in 1897, Joseph travelled to Washington to petition President McKinley. He paraded with Generals Howard and Miles in New York during the dedication of Grant's Tomb, and appealed once more to be returned to his Wallowa home.

In August 1899, Joseph revisited his Valley of Winding Waters for the first time in twenty-two years. He was treated kindly, but found no land available to his people. Joseph returned in June, the following year, with Indian Inspector James McLaughlin. While Joseph tearfully attended his father's grave, and gazed into the reflections of Wallowa Lake, McLaughlin reported that the Nez Perce's return there would be impractical. Joseph met President Roosevelt in 1903, and visited the Carlisle Indian School, Pennsylvania on his journey home, where he graciously met General Howard. The following year he sadly addressed a Seattle audience:

Today my heart is far away from here. I would like to be in my old home in the Wallowa country. The white father promised long ago that I could go back to my home, but the white men are big liars. That is all.

On 21st September 1904, the great Nez Perce headman suffered a heart attack while sitting beside the fire in the tipi at Nespelem that he still preferred to the white man's house. He was buried at Nespelem, where a monument now stands. Dr Edwin Latham suggested that Joseph 'died of a broken heart'. Four years before his death, Chief Joseph had expressed the lifelong wish for which he had fought so persistently and waited so patiently:

My heart is in the Wallowa Valley, and I want to go back there to live. My father and mother are buried there. If the government would only give me a small piece of land for my people in the Wallowa Valley, with a teacher, that is all I would ask.

Chronology of Events

Bibliography

In addition to the books listed below, a number of articles in periodicals are worthy of attention including 'Chief Joseph's Own Story' in the *North American Review* of April 1879, 'Chief Joseph' in the *National Geographic Magazine* of March 1977, and 'From Where the Sun Now Stands' by Bruce Wilson in the 1960 edition of *Omak*.

Beal, M.D. *'I Will Fight No More Forever'* University of Washington, 1963.

Brown, D. *Bury My Heart at Wounded Knee* Barrie & Jenkins/Pan, 1970.

Capps, B. *The Great Chiefs* Time Life, 1975.

Catlin, G. *North American Indians* Dover, 1973.

Gay, E.J. *With the Nez Perces* University of Nebraska, 1981.

Gidley, M. *With One Sky Above Us* Webb & Bower, 1979.

Gulick, B. *Chief Joseph Country* Caxton, 1916.

Holloway, D. *Lewis & Clark* Weidenfeld & Nicolson, 1974.

Josephy, A.M. *The Patriot Chiefs* Viking, 1961.

Josephy, A.M. *The Nez Perce Indians & Opening of the Northwest* Yale, 1971.

McLuhan, T.C. *Touch the Earth* Abacus, 1973.

McWhorter, L.V. *Yellow Wolf* Caxton, 1940.

Swanton, J.R. *Indian Tribes of North America*, Smithsonian Institution 1952.

Utley, R.M. *Bluecoats and Redskins* Purnell, 1973.

Illustrations

Colour plates by Richard Hook

Line illustrations and maps by Chartwell Illustrators

Photographs and other illustrations courtesy of: Idaho Historical Society (pages 15, 21, 27 and 37); Museum of the American Indian, Heye Foundation (page 11); National Archives, Washington (pages 4, 41 and 44); Royal Ontario Museum (page 7).

Index

Page numbers in *italics* refer to illustrations.